EAST ANGLIAN CRAFTS

EAST ANGLIAN CRAFTS

NORMAN SMEDLEY

B. T. Batsford Ltd
London

First published 1977
Copyright © Norman Smedley 1977

Set in 10 on 12 pt Linotype Pilgrim
Printed in Great Britain by The Anchor Press Ltd
and bound by Wm Brendon & Son Ltd
both of Tiptree, Essex
for the Publishers B. T. Batsford Ltd
4 Fitzhardinge Street, London W1H 0AH

ISBN 0 7134 0637 2

Contents

List of Plates

(*between pages 64 and 65*)

List of Drawings

THE LYF SO SHORT, THE CRAFT SO LONG TO LERNE,
TH'ASSAY SO HARD, SO SHARP THE CONQUERING.
Geoffrey Chaucer, 1340–1400

To Jack and Ena Carter,
whose help is always willingly given,
and gratefully acknowledged.

Acknowledgements

In compiling this record, I have had reason to be grateful to many individuals and institutions, and this indebtedness I acknowledge with thanks.

Ready help has been forthcoming from the County Record Offices at Ipswich and Bury St Edmunds, and from the County Libraries there and at Lowestoft. Facilities for study and the drawing of specimens have been received from my own former museums at Ipswich and Stowmarket (the Museum of East Anglian Life), the Bridewell Museum at Norwich, the Norfolk Museum of Rural Life at Gressenhall, the Colchester and Essex Museum, the Cambridge Folk Museum (Miss Enid Porter), the excellent little Rural Life Museum at Westleton (Caroline Campbell), the East Anglian Maritime Museum at Great Yarmouth, the Lowestoft and East Suffolk Maritime Society's Museum at Lowestoft (Commander R. G. Jenkins and Messrs V. E. Tuck, E. A. Pye and C. Chipperfield).

I am grateful to Major R. Mason, founder of the centre for Deben Craftsmen (carpentry, rush and osier weaving), H. and G. Boast of Rendham (wheelwrights), and a number of blacksmiths and farriers – Hector Moore of Brandeston, R. Hammond of Holton St Peter, Tom Dennis of Ditchingham, J. C. Cable of Barnby, R. Fulcher of Southwold, and John Cossey of Brooke.

My friend Wallace Morfey supplied an account of the processes involved in tanning; Leonard Aldous of Debenham, his nephew D. Balaam, and T. Smith, and Harry Loveday Ulph of Chelmsford (saddlers), and William Spence of Southwold and E. J. Catchpole of Kessingland (shoemakers).

Others who helped were Brian Palfrey (cooper); Frank Linnett of Hawkedon, Cyril Rackham of Bramfield and George John of Halesworth (thatchers); Frank Bird (rake and scythe-stick-maker) and his former colleague, Noël Cullum, together with Mr R. Hack, present owner of the Welnetham Woodworking Co., and Mrs J. W. Litchfield, former owner, who regenerated the craft when it was threatened with extinction; Arthur Lambert of Topcroft (hurdle-maker); Sidney Rous, of the Cove Bottom brickworks; Sam Avery, (flint-knapper); Keith Rackham, Arthur Sturman, Robert Denn and R. Baldry (stonemasons). W. G. Upcraft (net-making); Leslie Harrison of Cromer (crab-fisherman, and maker of crab-pots); Reg Reynolds and Norton Field (fish-curers); and Wilfred Clover (miller).

All the drawings have been made by me, from actual objects drawn to scale; the photographs for the plates are also mine, with the exception of the following, made available by the Suffolk Photographic Survey: II, V, VI, VIII, XVII, XVIII, XX, XXI, XXII, XXIII, XXXII, XXXIII, and the following made available by Mr Brian Palfrey: IX, X.

The selection has been made not so much with a view to providing uniform coverage of the crafts as to illustrate points of particular interest, as for example the difference between reed and straw thatching, and the developments made in the processes of rake- and scythe-stick-making, in which the older methods are illustrated by the drawings, the later by the plates.

Those interested in pursuing the matter further will find both drawings and photographs complementary to those in my earlier book, *Life and Tradition in Suffolk and North-East Essex*.

Introduction

In these days, when the term 'craftsman' has come to have a meaning only imprecisely related to its original sense, it is perhaps desirable that we should define it as it applies to the practice of traditional crafts; in industry, it is often used to denote one who has a specialized role as opposed to the general worker. This is by no means an accurate definition of the craftsmen with whom this book sets out to deal.

Craftsmanship is concerned with the selection of suitable natural products, and their adaptation to create objects of use to Man in his daily life. It has its origins in the remote past; our early ancestors gradually discovered that, from using literally 'sticks and stones', they could fashion these to be more effective for their purpose. Coupled with the development of greater skills must have been increased awareness of the beauty of the materials they used, and the forms they created. No one (with any sense of the aesthetic, at least) can handle some of the early implements of flint, and wood, without experiencing a sense of pleasure and wonder at their quality.

Gradually, one man here and another there would prove to be more proficient at some particular task than his fellows, and his services would be in demand to supply their needs as well as his own – and so craftsmanship was born.

So the craftsman came into being to provide for the needs of the community, to give service. But in so doing he was not without his reward, not only in payment, whether in cash or in kind, for his wares, but in something much more. He gained the great satisfaction of a job well done when the finished product served well the purpose for which it was made, and also the pleasure which comes from the creation of a thing of beauty; he had the joy of seeing the material in which he worked developing under his hand, and revealing its innate qualities. The true craftsman is a true artist; competent workmanship is allied to creative expression.

All this could not but have its effect on the make-up of the man himself; a sense of achievement brings tranquillity of mind, and stability of character; he was his own man. It is the fashion in these sophisticated days to decry and disparage the works of Longfellow, but his description of the village blacksmith rings true to those who have known him : He 'looks the whole world in the face for he owes not any man'.

Technological advance has brought many material benefits, but at a heavy price; it bids fair to result in the elimination of one of the staunchest pillars of our society – the craftsman.

Crafts fall into two main categories. Those which may be called 'village' or 'community' crafts were established where they could be readily available to those who needed them – in the village. Their number and character varied according to the local economy; in East Anglia, largely agricultural and pastoral, they were principally concerned with supplying the needs of the farming and fishing communities. It was common to find, within the confines of the village, a carpenter, blacksmith and farrier, wheelwright, saddler, cooper, cobbler, and in all probability a thatcher.

The other group consists of those sited most conveniently for the supply of the raw materials on which they were dependent; the potter must have a ready supply of suitable clay; osier-basket-maker and rush-weaver tended to seek out riparian localities, where conditions were favourable for the growth of willow, rush and reed, and similar factors, proximity to woodland, governed the choice of site by the hurdle-maker, rake-maker, and others. The flint-knapper's choice was perhaps the most restricted of any. Some writers have had a tendency to classify crafts according to the material they use – timber, metal, stone, and so forth. This pattern is not followed here; it tends to separate crafts which are in practice closely allied; wheelwright and blacksmith are to some extent dependent on one another's services, and in fact it is by no means uncommon to find the two crafts merged, especially where two brothers work together.

Tools tend to remain as traditional in character as the crafts in which they are used, and to be simple in form. Some processes can be accelerated by the use of powered tools, but not without some loss of the quality characteristic of hand-worked products.

There are workers who do not fit readily into the categories suggested above. Travelling craftsmen (as for example the tinker) are a dying breed. Then there are those who, whilst retaining that strong sense of independence inherent in the make-up of the true craftsmen, are of necessity in the employment of others – the estate carpenter, the brewery cooper.

On large or isolated farms, it is not unusual to find that the farmer himself, or one of his men, has acquired the skills necessary to shoe a horse, or repair the teeth of a harrow, and that the equipment is to hand; even more frequently, nowadays, minor disorders of the tractor, plough, or combine-harvester can be carried out on the farm.

Family tradition remains a strong influence, and son follows father from one generation to another, often in spite of the improved educational opportunities and the greater mobility of modern transport, both of which have proved factors in the drift from the land. Fortunately, too, early records are treasured; the account books, sometimes of three or more generations, give a picture of changing conditions and the ever-rising cost of materials and labour.

Although the tools of his craft remain substantially the same as those of his father and grandfather, the craftsman is not blind to the benefits of change, and adjusts readily when the need arises. Two village smithies recently visited in Suffolk illustrate this. Welding was no longer dependent on developing the right degree of furnace-heat; but oxyacetylene cylinders were in evidence. An electric pump provided draught for the forge, replacing the cumbersome if picturesque hand-operated bellows; but the tyring-platform was still in place, and in use, for shoeing the wooden wheels of early drills still favoured by some local farmers.

More drastic change is represented by such enterprises as the firm of James Smyth and Sons (only recently closed down), makers of a famous series of drills, and originating in the wheelwright's workshop of the first James, who began work in 1798 at the age of twenty-three. Botwoods, of Ipswich, who were making carriages and coaches, and even rickshaws for the Far East, in Victorian and Edwardian days, are now motor salesmen. Such metamorphoses can be multiplied in craft after craft.

After some deliberation, it was decided that it would be impracticable, in a book of this size, to include every craft practised in the region; some, such as boat-building and sail-making, have passed rather into the category of industries, although they still give employment to craftsmen; pottery-making has, as it were, dichotomized, giving rise to a commercial enterprise using almost purely mechanical methods, and to the work of the artist-potter. It was also felt that justice could not be done to the main body of traditional crafts if space had to be given to such occupations as lace-making, corn-dollies, and the like. Had all these been included, it would not have been possible to go into such detail as has been made possible through the ready co-operation of the craftsmen whose work is described.

THE REGION

Our concern is with East Anglia, a region which seems to contract or expand according to the view of the individual historian or geographer, and to what premisses are used as a criterion.

Some years ago, when the idea was mooted of establishing an Open Air Museum for East Anglia,* it was necessary to decide on a definition, as the scheme entailed the removal and re-erection of characteristic buildings.

To some, East Anglia comprised Norfolk and Suffolk, and these alone; Essex was the land of the East Saxons. Others favoured the inclusion with these of Cambridgeshire, and there were even suggestions of extending to the south-west into Hertfordshire, and north of the Wash to include Lincolnshire. However, moderate counsels prevailed, and it was finally decided that Norfolk, Suffolk, Essex and Cambridgeshire formed a natural region, physically and historically; this plan has been followed here. In general, East Anglia as thus defined has a character which links these counties in a natural entity, essentially different from the other provinces of the country, yet possessing within itself minor variations which lend additional interest. Long may it retain its unique character, in the face of the increasing demand by industrial interests for more direct links with the east and south.

* The Abbot's Hall Museum of Rural Life of East Anglia, which had been planned as a series of village groups, each representing one of the counties included. From 1975, after administrative changes, the emphasis was altered to include aspects other than rural, and the financial situation precluded additions to the already erected groups of buildings.

In compiling this record, I have endeavoured to avoid repetition of the work of previous writers; wherever possible, I have talked to the craftsmen themselves, and seen them at work. This should ensure that the account I give is authentic. I have reason to be deeply grateful for much ready help, and hope that I have not unduly tried their patience or interrupted their work; if so, they have given no indication of it. This direct method of collecting information was described as far back as 1901, by the late Charles Partridge, perhaps the most notable and assiduous of the recorders of local history in Suffolk, as the 'oral tradition',* and the term has been adopted by later writers. it is something more, for the experience is visual as well as oral. The earlier workers had not the advantage, as I and others have had, of recording the conversations on tape, and the actions with the camera. This allows the writer to check at leisure. I have acknowledged this help earlier, and sincerely hope that I have omitted no one.

Most of the photographs are my own, though much of their quality is due to the expert processing of my friend Geoffrey Cordy; where I have used photographs from other sources, this is stated in the acknowledgements.

In making the drawings, I have followed the same principle as in a previous book;† all are drawn from actual specimens, to scale. Where they relate to a craft illustrated in the earlier book I have, wherever possible, drawn them from another source; if I have been unsuccessful in finding another specimen, the implement in question has been redrawn, often from another angle. This has an additional advantage, in that the two books will give wider coverage for comparison.

Once again, too, I am indebted to my wife, who has read and re-read the typescript, and helped with the index.

* *East Anglian Miscellany*, Vol. 1, 1901.
† *Life and Tradition in Suffolk and North-East Essex*, Dent, 1976.

I
The Carpenter

Every man to his trade; that of the carpenter has been essential since Man first began to fashion wood to his needs. Yet in most accounts of crafts and craftsmen, the carpenter fails to achieve a niche of his own, but is lumped with the wheelwright or some other worker in wood. Such treatment does scant justice to a craft which has a distinctive character of its own, has played a most important role in the past, and still serves a necessary purpose, though the type of work now most in demand might be dubbed 'joinery' rather than carpentry, for it is the 'smaller structures' of the dictionary definition which are needed today. Carpentry, in one or another of its many manifestations, will be with us so long as the earth produces its raw material – timber.

At least up to the seventeenth century, the houses of the people in general were built by the carpenter. It was his ingenuity which solved the problems involved in creating the timber framework which gave such stability, and such a long lease of life, to the vernacular buildings of those earlier periods. Many such a house still survives, with its original timbers, when bricks and mortar of much later foundation have perished.

Oak was the principal wood used in house-building; it is a long time growing, but the end-product is a strong timber capable of

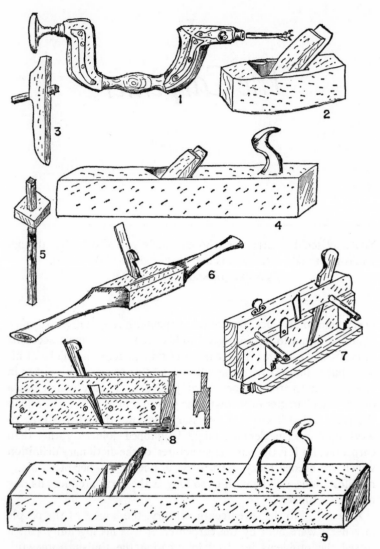

1 *The Carpenter's Tools*
  1. Brace 2. Smoothing-plane 3. Cutting gauge 4. Jack-plane
  5. Marking gauge 6. Fence router 7. Fillister 8. Moulding-plane
  9. Trying-plane (All 1/6 natural size)

withstanding the stresses and strains to which a building is subjected, both from without by the weather and within by its occupants. The oak-tree has a quality which is lacking in the softwoods; the very fibres which form the grain give it both its strength and its beauty.

The erection of a timber-framed house has been likened to that of the prefabricated buildings which were developed to meet a special need arising from the destruction of the Second World War. The comparison is a superficial one; in the one case, the simple assembly of factory-made units is all that is involved; in the other, the building is the work from beginning to end of one craftsman, or of a group working under his direction. The carpenter would often fashion the whole building in his yard, where seasoned timber was ready to hand. Each member was then numbered using Roman numerals, the same number also being incised on the beam to which it was to be joined. After completion, the framework was dismantled. and conveyed to its appointed site, where this form of indexing facilitated reassembly, which was not infrequently carried out with the aid of neighbours and friends. The character of the numerals is to some extent a guide to date; up to the sixteenth century, the figures were roughly gouged out, and tended to be large and coarse, but later the use of a sharp chisel gave a cleaner and often smaller type, although, of course, size was to some extent related to that of the timber. Another indication of date is given by the *scarf* joints used to join the longer timbers, e.g. sills and wall-plates.*

The common filling of the timber framework was wattle and daub. Pointed staves of oak or ash were inserted into holes bored with an auger into the upper member of each frame, and into a slot in the corresponding lower member; these were then interlaced with split hazel wands, thus forming a base on which was plastered a mixture of clay and dung, reinforced with horsehair.† As the use of bricks increased, the spaces were sometimes filled with brick nogging.

Weather-boarding was another early form of cladding for timber-framed buildings. Both oak and elm were used, attached by wooden pegs. The advent of cheap, machine-made nails, and the increasing employment of softwoods such as deal, related to the changed

* Cecil R. Hewett, *The Development of Carpentry.*
† R. W. Brunskill, *Illustrated Handbook of Vernacular Architecture,* Faber and Faber, 1971, pp. 56–62; and Harry Forrester, *The Timber-Framed Houses of Essex,* 1959, p. 35.

methods of building construction, ended the role of the carpenter as principal builder. His function was then to provide flooring, window- and door-frames, and other fitments. No longer did the very quality of endurance of the building depend upon his skill in planning and execution; his craftsmanship was diverted into other channels; his creative urge had to find other means of expression.

Related to his general joinery work was another specialization; he provided Man's ultimate requirement – the coffin. In all crafts there is a tendency to develop in one or other of two directions; he may become even more of a specialist – in the case of the carpenter this often meant becoming exclusively an undertaker; or he might amalgamate with another craft, such as wheelwrighting or coach-building. Increasingly today the carpenter, employed probably by a builder, is tempted to break away and set up on his own, to be his own master, and the master of others, emerging as a builder in his own right.

One effect of modern conditions is the disappearance of the imposing tool-chest of the traditional carpenter, stocked with every tool he might need. The change is particularly noticeable in the planes he uses. Gone are the stocks of beechwood, a pleasure in their own right to look upon and to handle. Gone are the long jack-plane which levelled the long pieces of oak and ash and elm, and the even longer try-plane, necessary to smooth over jointed timber; this latter was one of the family of jointer planes, culminating in the long jointer plane of the cooper, of such a length that it had to be reversed and supported on a stand, the wood being drawn over the plane, instead of the plane being pushed over the wood.

The tendency in these days is for less elaborate moulding, and that often produced by machine, so the seemingly endless array of moulding-planes, with blades to produce almost any conceivable variation of moulding, for cornices, door-frames, picture mouldings, frames, and the like, is now largely only to be found in the museums. Survivors, in the hands of some joiners at least, are the plough, with adjustable blade, for grooving, and the fillister, similar in form, for cutting rebates. The gauge, or scriber, too, seems to have retained something of its popularity.

Otherwise all work seems to be performed with planes of entirely metal construction. Fewer varieties are necessary; they seem to satisfy the present-day worker, but can they give the same pleasure in handling? Would they, in fact, prove their superiority, or even equality, given the same tasks as their predecessors. In receiving sets of tools for research and as additions to museum collections, the writer has been impressed by the evident regret with which the old craftsman parted with them, perhaps in some measure due to the fact that some of them had been used by his father and grandfather before him.

No doubt the modern tools have their advantages; they need less care for their maintenance. One carpenter pointed out that the synthetic handle of his chisel could be struck with a hammer without fear of damage, whereas the same treatment meted out to a wooden handle would fray it and eventually destroy it; a mallet was necessary; but it was a thing purely of utility, and not of beauty.

There is one activity in which the old tools may sometimes be a necessity: the restoration of antique furniture. The quality of their workmanship is such that it can only faithfully be reproduced, in some cases at least, by the use of the tools which went to its original making.

II
The Wheelwright

. . . while any man able to make a wheel knew enough to be a carpenter, on the other hand a carpenter could not do wheelwright's work, for lack of apprenticeship.

GEORGE STURT, *The Wheelwright's Shop* (1923)

When George Sturt wrote these words, he was purporting to reflect the general prejudice of wheelwrights in relation to carpenters, but he makes it plain that it was a view which he shared. His book is generally regarded as the wheelwright's Bible, and although the picture he gives is a true one, it needs some modification when applied to East Anglia. Sturt had succeeded to a business established in a town of some size; most of the East Anglian wheelwrights were village craftsmen working on their own, or with one partner and perhaps an apprentice.

His somewhat scornful appraisal of the work of the carpenters seems to have been in some measure due to dislike of the encroachment on his preserves by estate carpenters; the estate carpenter in East Anglia was as often as not a skilled wheelwright, who had to keep in running order a considerable number of wagons, tumbrils,

2 *The Wheelwright's Tools – I*
  1. Barking-iron, barker   2. Small barking-iron for 'wrongs' (branches)
  3. Axe   4. Draw-knife   5. Saw-pit 'dog', to retain logs in place   6. Adze
  7. Ring-'dog', for manipulating timber, by means of a pole passed through
  the ring   8. Froe, river, fromard, frower, thrower   9. Boxing-engine
  10. Jarvis   11. Bruzz   12. Gouge   13. Axle-pin lifter   14. Router, 'old
  woman's tooth'   15. Taper-auger   16. Compasses   17. Shell-auger
  18. Tyre-lever   19. Spoke-'dog'   (Nos 3, 7, 11 and 16 : 1/6; remainder :
  1/12)

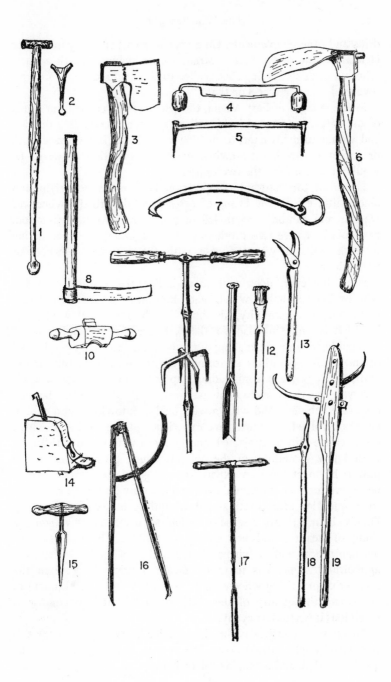

drills and other implements. On a visit to a carpenter's yard on the
Henham estate of the Earl of Stradbroke, a chance remark about a
wheelwright's stool lying about called forth the immediate comment:
'I've made many a wheel on that!'

In the villages of East Anglia, the wheelwright carried out much
of the carpentry needed in his village and the surrounding district,
and would turn his hand to making a scythe-stick, a corn-scuppit,
or a masher for home-brewing, when the occasion arose; so he
would often combine the two crafts.

The need for constant co-operation between wheelwright and
blacksmith, e.g. in the fitting of tyres or strakes to the wheels of
wagons and tumbrils, again led in many cases to amalgamation,
particularly where two brothers worked together, one specializing
in each skill, as was the case with the Plummer brothers of
Somersham.

Sturt, however, does well to underline the versatility of the
wheelwright, a quality which made him an indispensable member
of the village community, his shop, like the forge, vying with the
local inn as a meeting-place for the exchange of gossip and news.

Possibly because the making of the wheel is the most complicated
of the many operations performed, it has given the name to the
craft, but it conveys a misleading impression of the range of work
involved, for the wheelwright makes not only the wheels, but the
complete vehicle – and what a wide field of knowledge and experience is involved. He must have experience of the strains to which
each vehicle will be subjected, and know how to counter them; he
must know something of the animals which provide the motive
power; he must have an expert knowledge of the timbers which
best serve for each individual part, and not only be able to recognize
their qualities after cutting and trimming, but whilst growing.
Finally, he must have a sense of design, for a well-made wagon is a
thing of beauty, and not merely of utility. The extension of
mechanization, and the virtual disappearance of the horse from the
agricultural scene, has naturally meant a great decrease in the
number of practising wheelwrights, but a few still carry on, and to
appreciate the quality of the craft to the full it is necessary to
recall it as it was in its heyday.

An important task was the right choice of timbers, and for this
the wheelwright would scour the woods, marking trees of the
quality needed, and arranging for their purchase, often years before

they would be cut down. When the time came for felling, the gang would proceed first to strip the bark, using bark-peelers or 'barkers', varying in size from about two feet or so in length to a few inches, according to whether they were to be used for the 'right wood', the trunk, or the branches, the 'wrongs'. Winter-cut wood was not barked before felling; the bark would be hard and dry, and so would be both heart- and sap-wood. Spring cutting was to be preferred, and the bark, in the case of oak, would be sent for use by the tanners.

When the branches had been removed, the trunk was lashed underneath the 'timber-jim' (in Suffolk – more usually 'timber-jill' in Norfolk), and transported to the wheelwright's yard. These vehicles might have wheels as much as eight feet in diameter, and even so the axle was built with an upward curve between the wheels to give more room, in order to avoid the great trunks trailing on the ground. It was the gigantic size of some of the wheels which gave the cart yet another name – 'pair-of-wheels'; it was also known as a 'timber-drag'.

In the yard, each piece was carefully studied to ensure that the fullest use could be made of it; for example the natural curve of the grain might indicate suitability for shafts. After careful marking with the 'race', a special knife with a recurved point, it was handed over for the attention of the sawyers. The trunk was laid, manoeuvred into position by 'purchase' or ring-'dog', and supported by struts or rollers, over the saw-pit, and held in place with 'dogs'. (A nineteenth-century entry in the account book of William Clouting, blacksmith, of Boyton, Suffolk, is for 'turndown dorgs' supplied to James Fairhead, the local wheelwright.)

The pit-saw is an impressive tool, perhaps ten feet in length, with a long-necked 'tiller'-handle, attached transversely to the head of the saw, and operated by the top-sawyer, who straddled the log. Below, in the pit, was the bottom-sawyer, who attached a 'box'-handle to the end of the saw, and whose task it was to help the upward stroke, and to keep the saw oiled as required. His was an unenviable job, with sawdust pouring down on his upturned, sweat-streaked, face. The saw was not cross-cut, but worked only on the downward stroke. A number of cuts would be made before easing the log forward on the rollers, to save unnecessary movement.

Another saw, used by two men in much the same manner as the pit-saw, but above ground, is the frame-saw, employed more particularly for cutting the blocks from which the felloes of the

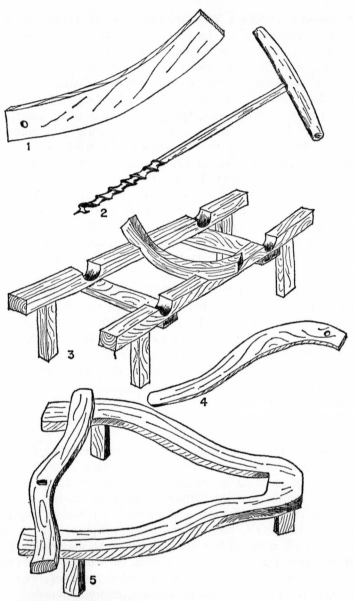

3   *The Wheelwright's Tools – II*
    1. Pattern for felloes   2. Spiral auger   3. Felloe-horse, with felloe in
position   4. Pattern for hames   5. Wheelwright's stool, cut from a natural
branch (Nos 1 and 4 : 1/12; 2 : 1/6; 3 and 5 : 1/16)

wheels are fashioned. It has varied little in general form since Roman times, and scarcely at all since Jan Weenix (*c.* 1600) engraved his representation of its use, depicting the Christ Child as top-sawyer, with Joseph as assistant, two angels manoeuvring logs, and the Virgin busy with a spinning-wheel.*

After the initial cutting by the sawyers, the timber was stacked, with spacers between the logs to allow free passage of air, and left for seasoning, often for several years, as many as ten in some cases. Sturt tells of nailing end-strips to prevent drying out and warping, but the usual practice in East Anglia would seem to have been to smear the ends with cow-dung to protect them from the extremes of the weather.

Since the wheel gave the craft its name, and because too it illustrates so well the care needed in selecting the right timber for each purpose, the making of a wheel seems to present a suitable subject to begin a survey of the wheelwright's work. Each part of the wheel has to make its particular contribution to the efficient performance of the vehicle.

The gait of the horse, with alternating movements of all four legs, conveys a rocking motion to the vehicle which it draws, and the effect of this must be counteracted in building the wheel. The full impact of the stresses caused is felt by the nave, and it has been found that elm, with its sinuous grain, can best combat this; from whichever direction the strain may come, there is a fibrous 'rope' to receive it.

The whole weight of the wagon and its load must be supported by the spokes; great strength is needed, and what better to supply this than oak? Finally the whole wheel must be bound together by a rim of felloes (*fellies* to the wheelwright), and for these ash provides the necessary adaptability. In the older wagons the axle-arms were of beech, a tough wood capable of standing up to the wear of the revolving hub.

All these measures, however, would be insufficient to prevent the collapse of the wheel due to side-rock, and the answer has been found in the element known as 'dish', by which the hub is sunk inwards in relation to the general plane of the wheel. In order to ensure that the spokes are vertical, however, when they meet the ground, the axle arm must be sloped slightly downward and forward. This has an added advantage, in that it causes the upper half

* Reproduced in W. L. Goodman, *History of Woodworking Tools*, Bell, 1964.

of the wheel to slope outwards, allowing for greater width of the body of the wagon, and avoiding any chance of the wheels scraping the sides.

The nave is turned on the great lathe, an imposing machine with a free-standing wheel of considerable size, turned by hand. In earlier times, shaping was carried out by means of the axe and adze. Next the block is secured on the stool, and the position of the spokes fixed with the compasses. The first hole was bored with the auger, continuing right through the block, in order to ensure that no error should be made in the number of spokes, which must be even; each felloe was driven on to two spokes. The writer has come across an instance of an error, no doubt made by an apprentice, in which an odd number of mortices had been cut; this resulted in one felloe having a single spoke, thus weakening the wheel. The mortices are cut out with a mortice chisel, and finished with a *bruzz*, a chisel with blade turned at right angles down the middle. Before this can be done, however, allowance must be made for the dish, by means of the spoke-set gauge; generally this is a strip of wood with a graduated series of holes into one of which may be inserted a strip of whalebone at a distance calculated according to the length of the spoke. This gave a 'sighting' on the point at which the mortice must be cut, at an angle to ensure the correct amount of dish. The proximal end of the gauge was screwed into the centre of the nave block, so that the gauge could be rotated as each mortice was marked. H. W. Baldry, of Horham, Suffolk, used a home-made *trammel*, a sliding gauge of wood, to mark off the length of the spokes. In the workshop of the brothers Boast, of Rendham, Suffolk, were a number of spoke-set gauges of a more primitive make than that described; they had pegs of wood, not whalebone, and were of different sizes, not adjustable.

Wood for the spokes was cut to approximate size by splitting with the *river* (*froe, fromard, frower, thrower*), an implement with blade set at right angles to the haft, which was held vertically so that the blade rested on the log to be split; it was then struck with a mallet. The spokes were next shaped with the axe, a remarkable tool with blade bevelled on one side only, and notched near the haft, to allow it to be gripped close by the head; it was used rather as a chisel than an axe and allowed of surprisingly delicate work. Smoothing was carried out with the *jarvis*, a plane with hollowed blade, but this seems to have largely gone out of use in East Anglia, only one having been found in the course of a number of visits to wheelwrights; the final finish was given with the *draw-shave* and *spokeshave*.

Blocks for the felloes were roughed out at an early stage, and left to season; they were then shaped with axe and adze, to conform in size to patterns kept in readiness, hanging on the walls of the shop, for the size of the felloe could be determined in advance according to the size of the wheel of which it formed a precise section. If the wheels were to be shod with strakes, the number of spokes would be twelve (rear) and ten (front), and the felloes respectively six and five; this means that the wheel would be less divided than when a hooped tyre is to be fitted (fourteen spokes and seven felloes (rear) and twelve spokes and six felloes (front)). The reason for this difference is that the straked wheel receives less support. As a further means of giving strength, the tongues which enter the felloes are squared in the case of a wheel with strakes, whilst rounded tongues are sufficient where a hooped tyre is used. Extra dish is given when the hooped tyre is shrunk on to the wheel. The fitting of tyres or strakes is, however, rather the concern of the blacksmith, and will be dealt with when we come to consider his craft.

Before the wheel could be 'hung' on its axle, the nave must be 'boxed' or fitted with an iron sleeve. For this the normal practice was to use the *boxing-engine*, a handled rod which was slotted through the central hole of the nave, held in position by three prongs top and bottom. An adjustable blade on the rod cuts away the sides of the hole until it is of the right size to take the sleeve. In some cases this process is still carried out with the gouge. The sleeve has lugs to prevent it rotating, and mortices to take these are cut with the *bruzz*.

As the spokes are beaten into the nave, they are pulled into place with the *bucker*, which is nothing more than a conveniently curved branch; a more sophisticated tool is used to brace the spokes so that the felloes can be driven on – the *spoke-dog* or *lever-type*. The forward edge of the spoke is chamfered so that in section it is ovate; the rear must be left round and strong to take the strain, but throughout the building of wagon or tumbril all surplus wood is shaved away to reduce weight so far as this can be done without impairing strength.

The felloes are held together by dowels inserted into their ends. Hugh Boast of Rendham pointed out the *shell-auger* as the implement

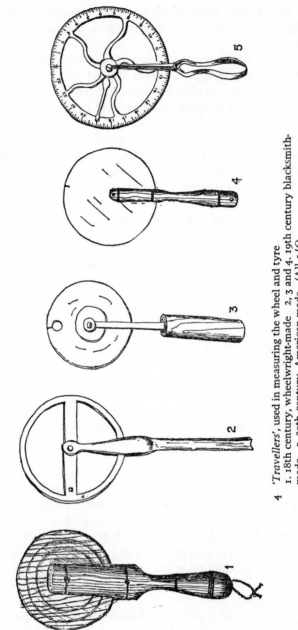

4 *'Travellers'*, used in measuring the wheel and tyre
1. 18th century, wheelwright-made 2, 3 and 4. 19th century blacksmith-
made 5. 20th century, American-made (All 1/6)

used for this, though a photograph taken in the mid-nineteenth century in the yard of a Suffolk wheelwright shows the *spiral auger* in use.

Finally, to hold the wheel firmly in position, a section is cut out of the nave to allow a lynch-pin to pass through into the arm of the axle; the piece removed is neatly replaced, with a latch to secure it.

If the wagon is primarily intended for farm-work such as harvesting, large wheels are an advantage; five feet or more for rear wheels is common in East Anglia, with four feet or so for the front wheels, but this makes turning difficult without some form of accommodation, and provision is made by cutting a 'waist' into the side of the wagon to allow more room for the front wheel to turn. For road-wagons, which may need to turn corners in narrow streets, the problem is solved by making the front wheels much smaller, to turn completely beneath the body. Some East Anglian wagons have wheels up to six feet in diameter, but this is almost the maximum for convenience of loading, when sheaves of corn have to be thrown up from ground level.

The track, the outside measurement from rim to rim of the wheels, varies somewhat, but six feet is usual; it was necessary to standardize this to some extent when deep ruts worn in muddy lanes during wet weather can become iron-hard under the summer sun or winter's ice.

Another farm vehicle made by the wheelwright was the tumbril. This was a two-wheeled cart, intended largely for carrying loads which could easily be handled by one man, e.g. the harvesting of root crops, and the carting of manure. The wheelwright's solution to single-handed working was the provision of a tipping mechanism, so that the load could be readily deposited at the end of the trip. The earliest form in East Anglia was one in which the body was secured to the shafts by a 'toe-bar', which passes through two iron loops on the shafts, and is prevented from being dislodged by an iron pin. When the toe-bar is removed, the body can be tilted back, allowing the contents to slide out. In order to facilitate this, the bottom was long-boarded, that is, the boards ran the length and not across the breadth of the cart. This method of construction was costly, as it entailed the addition of 'keys' nailed across the sides and summers of the bottom frame to take the floor-boards; it was therefore usually avoided in larger vehicles, such as wagons, where in any case there was less need for it. Even in the tipping-carts, or tumbrils, it became unnecessary when the importation of deal from Norway in the later years of the ninteenth century provided a smooth, planed surface, in contrast to the rough-sawn elm of earlier times.

Later variants of the tipping mechanism were the pivoted wooden bar, which could be turned to release the body to allow tipping and not removed like the toe-bar – an iron version of the same, and finally a vertical bar with holes which could be pegged to regulate the degree of tipping.

East Anglia produced a version of the tumbril capable of conversion to a harvest wagon by the addition of a fore-carriage; the shafts were removable by the withdrawal of an iron pin by which they were secured to the soles; the fore-carriage was then bolted in place, and the shafts attached to this, doubling the length available for the load. Because of its dual nature, it was known as the *hermaphrodite wagon*. The named proved a little too much for the local inhabitants who, in Suffolk at least, christened it *morphey*. On using this term recently to a Norfolk blacksmith, the writer was sharply corrected. Here it was *morphadite* or *morphradite*, and, in other parts, *hamphrodite*. Most of those on the Suffolk–Norfolk border, where it was most in use,* were made by W. E. Wigg and Sons of Barnby in Suffolk, or by G. R. Briggs of Ellingham in Norfolk, who worked for many years for Wiggs. A few of these wagons still survive, but for the most part in museums, or as treasured relics, rather than for use.

As has already been noted, however, the rural wheelwright was almost invariably called upon for many tasks other than the making of wagons and carts. A rare type of plane, the *router*, known locally as the *old woman's tooth*, was used to cut the grooves in the side planks of the steps made for use in barns and mills. The *corn-scuppits* used for shovelling grain were fashioned from a single piece of willow. On a visit to the twin brothers Hugh and Geoffrey Boast, whose wheelwright's shop stands just across the road from the churchyard at Rendham, the writer was told that only on the previous day they had made a coffin, perhaps to find a resting-place a stone's throw from the place where it was made.

Wheelwrights are now few and far between, but to a limited extent the craft, like those of the thatcher and the farrier, has been kept alive by a revival of interest in relics of an earlier age. Collectors of vintage vehicles – governess carts, dog-carts, gipsy-wagons – bring

* Although it was used to some extent in Lincolnshire and as far as South Yorkshire, and westward in Hertfordshire.

them to be restored to their former glory and a roadworthy state. It is by no means unusual for the wheelwright to be asked to repair the wheel of a Smyth drill, still a favourite with many a farmer.

In many cases, families or firms of wheelwrights have simply adapted to changing demands by developing into agricultural engineers, or distributors and repairers of motor vehicles. An Ipswich firm of this latter sort had early catalogues showing them to have been builders of coaches and carriages, and even of rickshaws for the Far Eastern trade. So craftsmanship has degenerated into salesmanship. Even at the time when George Sturt was writing, over half a century ago, he was deploring the fact that the spirit of comradeship which had animated his wheelwright's shop in its heyday when he, the master, could call every one of his fellow-workers friend, was disappearing in the new world of 'them' and 'us'.

III
The Blacksmith & Farrier

The smith, a mighty man is he,
With large and sinewy hands:
And the muscles of his brawny arms
Are strong as iron bands.
HENRY WADSWORTH LONGFELLOW (1807–1882)

In these sophisticated days, when poets, like other artists, are more concerned with creating a vehicle for their own feelings than in faithful representation of the subject, Longfellow's verses will no doubt be dismissed as sentimental. Written at a time, however, when the artist's concern was to present a true picture, and when the blacksmith was a worthy and indeed indispensable member of the community, the lines have a ring of absolute conviction. The smith filled a significant role from the earliest discovery of the possibilities of iron for weapons and tools.

Carpenter and wheelwright were concerned with the exploitation of timber, product of a living, growing organism. The blacksmith's raw material was of a very different nature, a substance derived from the very rocks of which the earth is formed – a substance capable, by subjecting it to powers of yet another element, fire, of being moulded and fashioned for the service of Man. Moreover, few of the creations of the workers in wood could be brought to completion without resort to the services of the smith. This was especially the case with the wheelwright; he and the blacksmith were mutually dependent in much of their work, at least during the period when horse-power was in truth what its name implies.

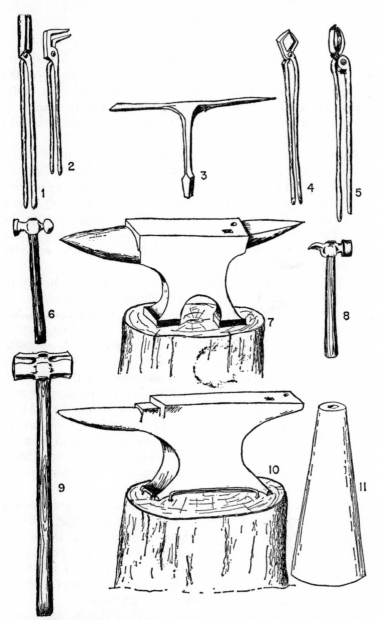

5   *The Blacksmith's Tools – I*
   1. Tongs, hollow-mouthed   2. Tongs, 'duckbill' or lipped   3. Bick-iron.
   mandrel   4. Tongs, 'box'   5. Tongs, pincer-lipped   6. Hammer, ball-pein
   7. Anvil, double-bick   8. Hammer, shoeing   9. Hammer, sledge   10. Anvil
   11. Floor-mandrel, 'sugarloaf' mandrel   (No. 3 : 1/6; No. 11 : 1/24;
   remainder : 1/12)

It was not only, however, in the provision of tyres for the wagons and tumbrils built by the wheelwright, nor in his capacity of farrier, that the blacksmith fulfilled his role in the life of the village. The farmer came to him for shares for his ploughs, blades and bails for his scythes, tines for harrows, and every member of the community sought his services at one time or another to make this – and repair that.

Blacksmiths seem to be especially conscious of the value of family tradition, probably because theirs was a craft which tended even more than most to pass down from father to son, and many of them have kept the account books of past generations, affording to us a most valuable picture of their work, and the changes wrought by time. The craft has a language of its own, and we are only just in time to get an accurate interpretation from the oldest surviving members of the fraternity.

Before giving an account of the work of the smith, it may be helpful to describe some of the apparatus and tools used, though some can best be left to be defined in relation to their function. We shall find some variation in nomenclature; many East Anglian craftsmen are not familiar with the names used in standard works on the subject; some working in areas separated by only a few short miles, in the same county, have different terms for the same tool. A case in point is the *swage* (*swedge* locally). The standard description is of a hollowed bar on a short neck which fits into the tool-hole of the anvil; metal to be bent may be beaten into it, or used in conjunction with a *top-swage*, rodded, it may be used to form the hot metal into a cylindrical bar, by striking with a hammer. Some smiths accept the regular designation; one called it a *hollowing-iron*; others had no special name for it.

One Suffolk smith used the term *swedge* for a small *hardy*, known in another county as a *heel-cutter*, for tapering off the heel of a horseshoe. A Norfolk smith set a *hardy* of standard size in the tool-hole of the anvil, placed the red-hot shoe over it, and cut off a piece of the heel; he called the *hardy* a *swedge*; so it is not safe to be dogmatic. The *fuller* resembles the *hardy*, but the edge of the blade is rounded; it is for beating out and lengthening metal.

The life-force of the forge is the hearth, a simple platform of brickwork, with a shallow pit to accommodate the furnace. At the rear is the chimney, hooded to control the draught. Behind, or sometimes above and to one side, is the bellows, either cylindrical

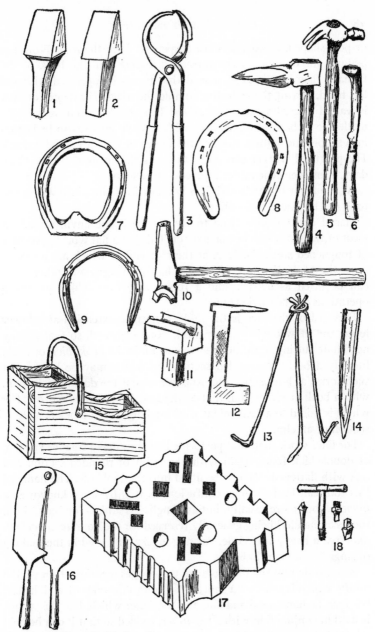

6 *The Blacksmith's Tools – II*
1. Fuller 2. Hardy (also known as 'swedge' or swage) 3. Hoof-parer,
modern 4. Punch 5. Hammer, shoeing 6. Hoof-cleaning knife
7. Bar-shoe 8. Shoe for draught-horse (near hind-foot) 9. Shoe for hack
10. Top-swage 11. Bottom swage 12. Buffer 13. Tripod 14. Punch,
pritchall 15. Farrier's tool-box 16. Castrating-clamp 17. Swage-block
18. Frost-nails and 'tap' (Nos 13, 15 and 17 : 1/12; remainder : 1/6)

or pear-shaped, at floor level or suspended from the roof. From the bellows the draught passes through a *tuyere* into the back of the furnace. The handle is so placed that it can be operated with the left hand, leaving the right free to hold the tongs. The degree of heat is varied according to need; a red heat renders iron sufficiently malleable to be bent or twisted; with a white heat it can be beaten into shape, and with a still greater degree of heat it can be welded. The practised worker can judge this at sight. In most forges, these days, a small electric motor replaces the bellows.

At the front of the hearth is a brick or iron tank, into which the tools can be placed for cooling.

Placed conveniently close to the hearth is the anvil, on which most of the work will be carried out. This has a flat working surface of toughened steel, the *face*, at the rear end of which are a square hole, the *tool-hole*, into which the hardy, swages, and other tools can be fitted as needed, and a round hole over which punching operations can be carried out.

Forward of the face is the table, a narrow extension at a lower level, and of wrought iron or steel, not toughened, so that it may not blunt cutting tools. Beyond this again is the *beak*, *bick* or *beck*, literally a beak, of rounded section, on which may be beaten out such forms as horseshoes, etc. Another type is the *double-bick anvil*, with a beak at either end, that at the rear being flatter on top. The whole is raised to a convenient working height on a block, usually a section of an elm.

For finer work than that performed on the anvil a smaller version, of double-bick form, again with one point of rounded section and one with flattened top, can be fitted into the tool-hole. The name of this tool can lead to some confusion, as it is by some known as a *mandrel*, but more usually, in East Anglia, as a *bick-* (or *beck-*) iron, the term mandrel being generally reserved for the *floor-* or *sugarloaf-mandrel*, a heavy iron cone, varying in size, and used in the making of rings, e.g. for cart hubs.

Also fitting into the tool-hole are the swages mentioned above, the *hardy*, which is in effect a short chisel, on to the edge of which steel bar may be hammered and cut, and the *fuller* which, like the swage, is used in conjunction with a *top-fuller*, rodded so that it can be held whilst being struck with the sledge-hammer. This combination is used when it is necessary to spread and lengthen a bar; the surface is rendered wavy in the process, and has then to be flattened with the *flatter*, a tool of similar form to the top-fuller, but with a broader, rounder head. An interesting point emerged in conversation with a Norfolk blacksmith. Picking up a rodded fuller, he pointed to the handle, made from rod of round section which is wrapped two or three times round the head and drawn together and welded at the tip. 'This,' he said, 'is a *with*' (the local word for *withy* or *withe*). He explained that in much earlier times the handle had in fact been made from a branch cut from a sapling, and twisted to form a handle.

Another implement which provides a butt for metal to be beaten into various shapes is the swage-block, a thick heavy square of cast iron, the sides providing rounded or angled surfaces against which the metal can be set as it is struck with the hammer; in the face are holes of various shapes into which the hot metal can be driven.

The *cold chisel* is used for cutting cold iron, as the name implies; it is struck with the small hammer; the *hot chisel*, for hot iron, is longer in the shaft, and is used in the same manner. For heavier tasks, the *cold set*, with rodded handle, and the *hot set*, with wooden handle to guard against the heat, are used with the sledge-hammer. Punches, too, are rodded in the larger versions. Perhaps the most important aspect of the blacksmith's work, until recent years, lay in his services to agriculture. In addition to his work as farrier, with which we shall deal later, he had to maintain in working condition many of the implements of the farm. He played an essential part in the production of the wagons and carts used on the farm, making all the metal accessories for the wooden body and wheels built by the wheelwright. Just as the construction of the wheel calls for the utmost skill of the latter craftsman, so its *shoeing* demands expert knowledge; an error of judgment could reduce the carefully built wheel to a twisted wreck as the tyre is fitted. The implements used are ingenious, but simple; success rests on the expertise of the craftsman.

The older method used was *straking*, in which a number of plates were fitted on to the circumference of the wheel, one to each pair of felloes. The exact size could, of course, be determined before-hand, allowance being made for the fact that the strakes would be applied hot, and would therefore expand when placed in the furnace. They were cut off from the strip, cold, using the cold set and sledge-hammer, then heated until red-hot, when holes were punched, four or five at either end of the strake, for attachment to the felloes.

Careful measurement was essential to ensure that the holes were so spaced as to correspond exactly with those already punched in the felloes; the huge nails could not simply be driven through, as this would split the wood.

Before the final strake was put in position, a clamp known as a *samson* was secured over the joint between the last two felloes, and anchored to a nail which had been left projecting in each of the strakes on either side of the joint.* The samson was then tightened so as to close the last joint securely.†

It will be evident that, as the strakes were secured one at a time, the process would not, as in the case of hoop-tyring, help to produce *dish* in the wheel, so this had to be allowed for when assembling the wheel itself, as has already been indicated in the account of the work of the wheelwright.

Strakes had some advantages; several could be heated in the furnace at the same time; wear on one did not entail replacement of the whole set; they also gave some measure of grip in slippery, muddy conditions, much in the same way as does the tread of a motor-car tyre.

The blacksmith made his own nails; for straking or tyring there were *spekens*, large, flat-headed nails, the heads countersunk so that they would wear evenly as the tyre wore down. A die with holes of various sizes, bevelled down to shape the head, was used to fashion the nail. The blacksmith at Boyton in Suffolk recorded in his account book the supply to the local wheelwright of *speakons*, together with *turndown dorgs* (the iron *dogs* which held in place the logs over the saw-pit). A blacksmith at Framlingham made 'headed nails' for the wheelwright employed in the Parish Surveyor's Department; his brother, also a smith, called them *spikings*:

If anything, the fitting of a hoop tyre was a more complicated process than straking. The circumference of the wheel was measured, sometimes by running the wheel itself over the strip from which the

---

* Not, as seems to have been the case in Sussex, round a spoke and a nail. (George Sturt, *The Wheelwright's Shop*, C.U.P., 1923, p. 152.)
† The origin of the term, *samson*, is obvious. It is many years since straking was carried out, but recently a wheel was straked, as a demonstration, by Hector Moore of Brandeston, Suffolk. The writer was privileged to be present, and took photographs which are published in his book, *Life and Tradition in Suffolk and North-East Essex*, Dent, 1976, plates 32–8.

tyre was to be made, sometimes with the aid of the *traveller*. This was a small, handled wheel, sometimes of wood (probably made by the wheelwright), but more usually of iron, a simple plate or an open ring, made by the smith himself. A particularly sophisticated example, American in origin, is graduated in inches, and has a pointer to indicate the final mark, from which an accurate reading may be taken on the scale. On the more primitive instruments in general use, a cut in the edge of the traveller gives a starting point, and this is placed in line with the joint between two felloes. The operator walks round the wheel, placed horizontally on the stool, and counts the number of revolutions, making a chalk mark to note any excess. He then repeats the process on the strip to give the circumference of the tyre.

The strip is cut, and the ends *scarfed*, or thinned down by beating, in readiness for welding together. Then the strip is placed in the *tyre-bender*, a kind of 'mangle', which gives it the necessary degree of curve. The two scarfed ends are heated and beaten together. Welding completed, nail holes are punched in the hoop whilst it is still hot.

Before finally fitting, the inside of the newly made tyre is checked once again with the traveller (or *wheel-maker* as one smith called it), to ensure a correct fit.

Meantime, the wheel has been screwed down over the tyring-platform or *plate*. The pressure exerted by the central screw of the plate on the nave is responsible in some measure for effecting the right amount of *dish* in the wheel.

Now the tyre must be heated, sometimes over a ring fire specially laid for the purpose, at others by holding it vertically over the furnace, rotating it until the heat is evenly distributed; less frequently, the forge is equipped with an upright oven in which the tyre can stand vertically; one of these still exists, though now no longer used, at Belstead in Suffolk.

Tyres were made for the wheels of farm implements other than wagons and tumbrils, of course, and it is the popularity of some of these which has been responsible for a need for the blacksmith to keep in being the apparatus for this work. This is especially the case with the drill introduced by James Smyth and Sons in the nineteenth century. One such drill, purchased in 1830, was used until the owner decided to stop doing his own drilling, and to put the work out to contract. This was in 1964, and the drill served four generations of

the family. Others are still in use, and this point is well illustrated
by the following experience of the writer. Chancing to notice a
smithy when passing through a village on the borders of Suffolk
and Essex, it seemed an opportunity to examine the local state of
business. Inside the door was an oxyacetylene cylinder, which
seemed to suggest a change-over to agricultural engineering. Outside,
at the rear, was a tyring-platform. Surely this was no longer needed,
and might join the collections at the Rural Life Museum. The sug-
gestion was courteously received, but instantly rejected; the *plate*
was still doing active service – for tyring the wheels of Smyth drills.

The founder of the firm making these drills was himself a craftsman, James Smyth, who set up as a wheelwright in 1798, at the age
of twenty-three.* Two years later he laid the foundations of a
prosperous business by putting on the market an improved version
of a drill designed by a local rector, the Rev. Cooke of Semer.

Volumes have been written on the subject of the dialect of the
region, but they by no means cover the ground. The early account
books and ledgers, particularly perhaps those of the blacksmiths,
abound with terms which have so far not found their way into print.

Clinks were the rivets used when wood and iron had to be bound
together.

> To a Bean hoe Layd.
> To pick laid pick end & broad batg.
> To axletree Layd both ends Govt. Cart.
> To 5 new teeth & 2 end ones Layd to Garden rake & Socket mendg.

The process of *laying* was lengthening by adding fresh metal;
bating or *beating out* speaks for itself, as do the contractions.
Evidently the *pick end*, the pointed end of a pick or mattock, had
worn down and needed the addition of extra length to make it
serviceable, whilst the broad end, with adze-like blade, required
beating back into shape. The axletree of the governess cart had
worn down, so that the wheel fitted loosely; both ends needed
strengthening.

> To a hoop tire mendg. & bigng.
> large piece wt. 2 lb. laid on & put on fore wheel of van.

Bigng. (*biggening*) was, of course, to make bigger.

> To Scythe hanging on new stick.
> To Scythe hanging & bail mendg.

* P. J. O. Trist, *A Survey of the Agriculture of Suffolk*: Royal Agricultural
Society of England County Agricultural Surveys, No. 7, 1971, p. 180.

The *hanging* of a scythe was not a simple matter of fitting on a new handle; it had to be adjusted exactly to suit the individual user. This service was not performed by the scythe-stick-maker, but by the blacksmith. With the blade resting on the ground, and the *snead* or scythe-stick resting against the shoulder, the first hand-grip or *tack* was placed at the limit of the finger-tips. The second tack could then be adjusted by allowing the distance from elbow to finger-tips. If the scythe was then held with the first tack resting on the finger, it would balance at the angle of $45°$.

The *bail* was the iron hoop attached to the scythe to gather in the corn when mowing barley, which was left lying loose, and not bound into sheaves.

The *dibbles*, used for planting corn or beans, wore down by being constantly thrust into the earth:

To a pair of Dibbles Layd 3 oz. of Steel.

It was important to state the amount of metal used; this affected the cost of the operation.

A pair of 'Chaff Engeon' knives were supplied, and ploughshares made, together with other plough parts, notably the *foot*. This was an iron bar, of square section to fit the socket, and could be used as an alternative to the land-wheel of the plough, which ran over the surface, and tended to sink into clay in wet weather, making heavy going for the horses. The distal end of the foot was turned at right angles, and flattened, so that it would glide over the surface like the runner of a sledge.

Another item in constant demand was the *false link*. This was an open link, with the ends overlapping, which could be easily slipped in to connect a broken chain when ploughing.

Many blacksmiths actually made ploughs of their own design, as for example the Goldhanger Plough, made by the blacksmith of that Essex village, Warren, and later by Bentalls at Maldon.* Both the common plough and the *tom-plough*, used for opening up the trenches for potatoes, and for earthing them up,† were made; they

---

* A. F. J. Brown (*Essex at Work 1700–1815*, Essex Record Office Publications, No. 49, p. 41) states that 'the Goldhanger blacksmith made special ploughs for a local farmer called Bentall, who subsequently set up a factory at Heybridge'. The ploughs are still used on some Essex farms.
† P. J. O. Trist, *A Survey of the Agriculture of Suffolk*: Royal Agricultural Society of England County Agricultural Surveys, No. 7, 1971, p. 184.

must have entailed the co-operation of a wheelwright or a carpenter, as they are wooden ploughs.

The first iron plough ever to be introduced was made by a Suffolk blacksmith named Brand.*

In Suffolk, the 'East Anglian Plough' was made by Daniel Cameron at Bungay, and by his successor in the business, H. N. Rumsby.

At one time or another, almost every member of the community called on the blacksmith for help.

	s.	d.
To a faillie [faulty?] Grate narrowd & bars welding done twice .		4
To a Steel to Strike fire	.	3
To a hoop fittg & put on Keeler	.	1½
To 2 heters making to Ittalion Iron	.	6

and on December 24, perhaps in readiness for the Christmas festivities:

	s.	d.
To a very Stout handle making to frying pan	.	4
To poker Layd	.	8
To Lanthorn	1	6

– cheap at the price, as the windows were made of cow's horn pared down sufficiently to let the light through.

Undoubtedly the side of the blacksmith's work which is most readily conjured up in the public mind is farriery, for which his services are still in demand, at least as shoesmith; formerly it entailed a great deal more than this, and the older books on farriery are concerned entirely with the treatment of ailments. In these times perhaps most shoes are factory-made, and only fitted by the farrier, but there still remain smiths who scorn to supply anything which has not been made from the bar, in the smithy.

The first task, after a preliminary examination to assess the extent of the work to be done, is to remove the old shoe. The heads of the nails are sheared off with the buffer, and the shoe removed with the pincers. The hoof is cleaned with a special knife with the tip of the blade turned over at right angles. A Norfolk smith said, 'We used to make our own. You want two or three; you want a broad one, and you want a little narrow one – what we called a *searcher*.' He also said that the bone or horn handles of these knives became burnt

---

* Arthur Young, *A General View of the Agriculture of Suffolk*, 1813 : Reprinted by David & Charles, 1969, p. 32.

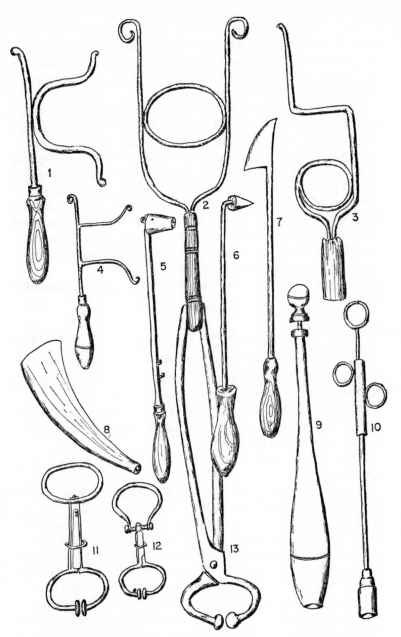

7 *The Farrier's Instruments*
  1, 2, 3 and 4. Horse-gags, farrier's gags, balling-irons   5, 6. 'Pin-firing' irons
  7. 'Strike-firing' iron   8. Drenching-horn   9. Ball-gun, wooden   10. Ball-
  gun, metal   11, 12. Bull-holders   (All 1/6)

away in time, and he used to replace them with iron. After cleaning, the hoof is pared where necessary to even off the surface with the *hoof-parer*, which rather resembles a pair of pincers with one jaw bevelled away to a sharp edge.

Then measurement is taken to determine the length of bar which will be required, and this is cut off with the cold set and sledge-hammer. The metal is heated in the furnace and beaten to the approximate shape of the hoof; then whilst still hot it is tried on the hoof. A great deal of smoke and a pungent smell of burning results, but no pain is caused to the horse; the hoof is horny, and not at all sensitive. After a number of trials, the shoe is ready for fixing, but first the nail holes must be punched. It is placed over the punch-hole of the anvil, and the holes tapped in with the *pritchell*. Then it is seated on the hoof, and the nails driven in with the *shoeing hammer*, and clinched by the forked beak of the hammer.

Entries in the farrier's ledger introduce us to yet more unfamiliar terms.

	s.	d.
To 4 shoes & Steeld. Grey hoby	2	4
To 2 shoes & 2 removes Tommy	1	6
Dec. 25. To an old Shoe & 1 remove Christmas day morning	.	3

Was the stress on the date the mark of a justifiable pride in a readiness to serve regardless of any inconvenience?

When a shoe showed signs of undue wear at one point, often the heel, it was removed and cut away sufficiently for a piece of steel to be welded into the weak spot.

Hoby or more usually *hobby* was the term for a pony (often spelt *poney*).

In the case of the horse 'Tommy', evidently two shoes were so worn as to need replacement; the other two were in sufficiently good shape but the hooves required some attention, so the shoes were removed and replaced after the hooves had been trimmed.

When three shoes were capable of surviving for a longer spell, but one was badly worn, this was replaced by an old one in rather better condition, in the hope of deferring the complete operation.

The above examples are taken from ledgers dating from the 1820s; the charge of about 6d. per shoe remained in force over a very long period, and had only risen to 7d. or 8d. by 1900. The Great War of 1914–18 brought a rapid increase, to 2s. 3d. per shoe in 1921. Then prices eased, and by 1936 a full set of four shoes was fitted for nine shillings. Recent years have seen a phenomenal increase, to £5 or more for the set. Prices were sometimes stated as for 'taken horses', implying that the shoeing was carried out at the smithy; more would be charged for a visit to the farm, taking along a portable forge, if the farm did not boast one of its own.

An entry in 1824 is for *ironing up* four pairs of *sales*, another word for *hames*. Both terms have an alternative spelling, – *sails* and *haims*. The wooden hames were made by the wheelwright, who kept a series of wooden patterns of different sizes. Careful details are noted of the requirements for each pair. The first pair was to have '2 eyes & bells & sheers & shoulder hooks & ringles & links wt. 5½', and the cost, five shillings, was the same for all.

Bits, too, were at one time made by the farrier, particularly those used for a special purpose, e.g. the keyed bit used in horse-breaking; the pendants titillating the tongue caused salivation, and this acted as an emollient to prevent chafing of the mouth by the unaccustomed bit.

A sudden cold snap would bring a demand for *ruffing* (roughing); the heels of each shoe were turned down to form *calkins*, to give a better grip on icy roads. When the time came for a new set of shoes, frost-nails might be put in some of the holes; these were large-headed nails with a wedge-shaped head. Larger frost-nails or frost-pins were made either with a square shank or rounded and threaded. The former required the punching of enlarged holes, and this was carried out over the punch-hole of the anvil, on which was first placed a *bolster* with square central hole, so as to prevent the shoe being bent during the operation of punching. For the threaded form, the holes were made bigger with a *tap*. These nails, too, were called *calkins*, and the process known as *calking*.

The farrier was frequently called upon to apply his special knowledge of the horse to the cure of its ailments. In fact, an entry in White's *Directory of Suffolk* for 1844 gives the designation 'Veterinary Surgeon and Shoeing Smith', and such publications as Day, Son and Hewitt's *Key to Farriery* (1896) were exclusively devoted to the treatment of ailments. The recipes were largely herbal, and a MS. notebook found amongst a bundle of documents from a north Suffolk farm showed by its dog-eared state that it had been much used. A number of recipes from this booklet, ranging from the treatment of the *nods* to a method of making a horse 'cover when he is unwilling', have been related in an earlier book by the present writer,* and need not be repeated here. Some are concerned with a means of giving control over a restive horse, and both farriers and horsemen on the farms claim, and apparently with some justification, to be able to exert considerable powers in this respect. The secret is closely guarded, but what has become almost a legend has grown up concerning the use of frogs and toads in this form of 'magic'. The following note was contributed to the *East Anglian Miscellany* in 1958:

At that day the villagers used to catch the creeping toads, not those that hopped, and, killing them, dig a hole and bury them; the ants would eat the flesh and leave the bones bare. These were placed in a running stream and if one bone 'strove against the stream' the said bone was kept and used as a charm. It was said that such a bone would be of use in stopping runaway horses on a waggon. I have heard such from a relative of mine now living in Ipswich; and, indeed, such was performed at Whatfield and Hadleigh by a man whose initials were F.T., and, again, by a man named Farrow, who lived at Elmswell, near Bury.

— W. Juby, Ipswich.

Weakness and spreading in the hoof are corrected by the *bar-shoe*, in which the heels are connected by a rod of iron. A further development of this is the *round-shoe*, a complete oval; tenderness is relieved by incorporating a leather sole. Various forms of the *farrier's gag* or *balling-iron* were fashioned, and used, by the farrier to force open the mouth when administering a *ball* or pill to a horse, or this could be literally 'shot' down with a *ball-gun*. Liquid doses, or powders, were given using a *drenching-horn*, an adapted cow's horn. Roughened teeth were filed down with the *horse-rasp*, and a 'wolf tooth', projecting into the cheek, beaten out with a toothed chisel and mallet. For an ordinary extraction, an instrument consisting of a stout rod with a curved jaw which tightened round the tooth as the rod was twisted, was used. Many blacksmiths kept handy a smaller version of this device, with which they would come to the aid of a friend suffering the pangs of toothache!

The following entry is taken from the ledger of a Framlingham farrier:

		s.	d.
1833. Jany. 10.	To dressing horse's foot	.	4
20.	To foot dressing	.	4
Feby. 8.	To Horse tooth drawer making	.	1½

The farrier dealt not only with horses, but with other farm

* *Life and Tradition in Suffolk and North-East Essex*, Dent, 1976.

animals. He made ox-shoes, two plates to each foot, to fit the cloven hoof. To prevent self-suckling, a common and troublesome habit, he co-operated with the saddler to produce a spiked collar, which made the practice uncomfortable; a smaller collar of the same pattern, fitted on the calf, helped in weaning, the points causing the cow to flinch away. Cattle, too, had to be given pills or other medicines. In their case the opening of the mouth was assisted by inserting the prongs of a *bull-holder* into the nostrils.

Lest we should forget, in our preoccupation with his work as farrier, we may remind ourselves, by a glance at his account book, that he might at any time have to turn aside to sharpen or *lay* mill-bills for the miller, to grind the butcher's cleaver or axe, to make a new *bail* for the dairymaid's pail, or mend or even make a kettle-trivet for the old lady in the cottage down the street.

IV

The Leather Crafts

And the Lord God made for Adam and his wife coats of skins and clothed them.

Genesis, Chapter III, verse 21

Whether we accept the Bible story literally, or prefer to rely on archaeological evidence, it is clear that from very early times Man has found the skins of animals an invaluable material, ready to hand, to be adapted to many of his needs. They have given him clothing; he has fashioned them into tents to give him shelter; he has stretched them over a wooden framework to provide boats for transport along the rivers and streams; they have provided harness for his horses and other beasts of burden, shoes to protect his feet, rugs and mats and handbags and suitcases. True, they are now being supplanted to some extent by man-made materials, but these are accepted as substitutes not because of their superiority but because they are relatively cheap.

At first, no doubt, skins were used in their natural state, and it was only by degrees that Man found, first, that scraping and sun-drying made them less likely to deteriorate, and then that by treatment with various fluids, and by manipulation, they could be rendered not only more lasting, but more supple and adaptable for fashioning into a variety of articles of use or ornament.

The preparation and use of leather have given rise to four distinct crafts: those of the tanner, who preserves the leather, or perhaps more accurately converts the skin into leather; the currier, who renders it supple and ready for use; the saddler, who has always performed more functions than his title implies; and the boot- and shoe-maker, or cobbler. The saddler may specialize; he may advertise himself as a saddler or saddler and harness-maker, or collar-maker, or any combination of these.

Tanneries were mostly to be found in the towns rather than the villages; the processes involved require considerable space for the accommodation of the necessary equipment; curriers, on the other hand, were to be found in many villages, and the craft was often combined with that of the shoe-maker. It is only in comparatively recent years that the work of the currier has become merged with that of the tanner, largely because modern methods produce leather suitable for use as it is supplied by the tannery, although the saddler still requires leather which has been rendered supple to a high degree, and additional processes may be needed to turn this out.

All four crafts have lost their former status in the rural economy, and their functions have altered. No longer are the services of the saddler needed to make harness for the draught horse to pull plough or harrow or drill, wagon or tumbril; the village cobbler no longer keeps the farm-worker dry-shod. But for the former at least the revival of interest in riding means a demand for saddle and bridle, and not only do mounting costs of petrol and heavy machinery seem to be turning the attention of some farmers to the possibility of reintroducing the earlier methods of tillage at least in certain cases, but there is evidence to show that land trodden by the horse keeps in better shape than that which is constantly subject to the pressure of the heavy tractor, though against this must be balanced the time factor and the increasing cost of labour.

We have become so accustomed to accepting the idea that old ways and old crafts are on the way out, that it came as something of a surprise, on visiting a recently revived Horse Fair, to see the number of saddlers there displaying their wares.

THE TANNER AND THE CURRIER

The first stage in the treatment of the hide is a thorough soaking in water, making it more amenable to the preliminary *fleshing* (the removal of the remnants of flesh and connective tissue from the interior of the hide), and capable of absorbing the solutions to be used in curing. It is then ready for *liming*.

This was formerly carried out in a lime-pit, beginning with a mild solution, which was *mended* every two days by the addition of fresh quicklime. The effect is to 'plump up' the skin, in which state it more readily takes in the tanning liquid, but before being subjected to this treatment it is once again washed; it is then cut up into suitable pieces, separating the *butt* (the middle section overlying the backbone) from the thinner sides. An earlier practice was to cut down the line of the backbone, dividing the skin into *sides*, and this is still necessary when the leather is to be used for harness, in order to obtain the length of strip needed. The work of removal from one tank to the next was formerly carried out manually, but the whole process has become more and more mechanized, the skin now being 'rocked' in a drum of the lime solution, and passed through mechanically to the washing drum, and so to the tanning vats.

The drums of tanning fluid are arranged in sequence, beginning with a weak, used mixture, the hide moving up to gradually stronger solutions at the top of the yard, and the drums moving down, so that the weakest solution is always at the bottom, and the new strong fluid at the top. All these processes are now performed automatically in the normal course, but there is still some demand for hand-tanned skins, and especially for 'hand-fleshed' leather, as it is considered, with some justification, that the machine tends to damage the fibre.

In the past, the tanning solution was made from oak bark, supplied by local timber merchants and carpenters,* and in addition oak was coppiced specifically for the purpose of maintaining a supply. All this is now past history; the ingredients for making up the tanning fluid are obtained mostly from overseas. The extracts arrive ready for use – *quebracho*, a hardwood tree native to South America (reputed also to be an effective febrifuge), *mimosa, valonia* (the acorn-cups of the Levantine Oak, *Quercus aegilops*) imported from Smyrna. These were ground in a mill, water added, in the days when the tannery mixed its own tanning preparation; they now arrive ready-ground.

The tanner treats the hide in order to preserve it – he transforms

* A. F. J. Brown, *Essex at Work 1700–1815*, Essex Record Office Publications, No. 49, 1969.

skin into leather. Further treatment is necessary before it is ready to be fashioned into harness by the saddler or made into footwear by the shoe-maker; this is now done in the tannery, but in earlier times was performed by a specialized craftsman, the *currier*; he was not infrequently also the shoe-maker, and statistics in the early directories show that curriers practised in many villages. In Suffolk alone, there were forty curriers listed in *White's Directory* for 1844; twelve were still working in 1904; eight in 1922. Fifteen years later no curriers appeared in the lists separately, but many tanners were shown as 'tanners and curriers'.

It was the development of machinery which was responsible for the virtual disappearance of the currier, for the manual process was an arduous task, requiring special tools and great skill. The tanned hide was washed and softened, scrubbed, and the residue of the tanning fluid squeezed out with a short, deep-bladed knife, the *sleeker*. Then the inner surface was further evened using a knife with blade turned at the edge at right angles to the face. The same tool was used for the splitting of the skin, for varied thicknesses of leather were used for different purposes. The leather to be used for the uppers of shoes and boots had been more lightly tanned than the rest of the hide, and was now split, to give a more pliant and supple leather. Split leather was also used for suede. The soles were made from the heavier *butt* leather, often untanned.

The actual process of *currying* consisted in working in to the leather a mixture of equal parts of beef tallow and cod-liver oil.

THE SADDLER

Reference has already been made, in the introduction to this chapter, to the specialization which was to be found within the saddler's craft, collar-makers and harness-makers sometimes following their own individual line of work to the exclusion of all else. This was a practice more generally to be found in the towns; the village saddler had to meet demands for services not only in these particular crafts but to cope with many other needs of the community. He made the harness for the horses which drew the wagons and ploughs and other farm implements, and the lighter breeds used in the traps, dog-carts and governess carts indispensable at that time for journeys near and far; he made saddles and bridles for the hacks and hunters; he furnished the leather pads to counteract wear on the shafts of wagons and carts.

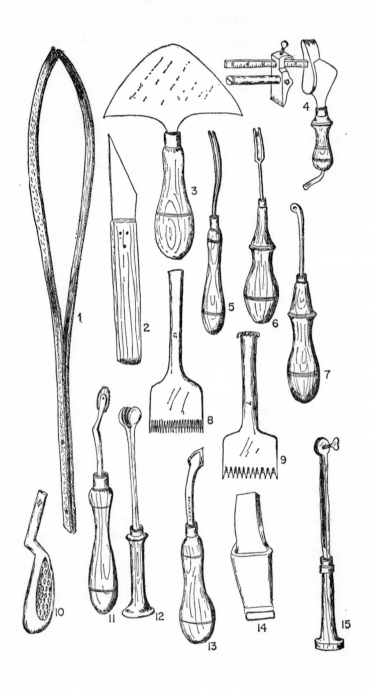

On the great estates, the sweeping lawns were cut and rolled using horse-drawn machines; the shoes of the heavy horses must not be allowed to cut up the turf as they trod it; so the saddler made boots for them to wear whilst performing this task. One Essex saddler was approached by the proprietor of a circus, and asked to make a set of similar but larger boots – for the elephant which had to tramp from town to town.

If the belt driving the threshing drum snapped, it was the saddler who was called upon to make a quick repair. When a calf refused to be parted from its mother's supply of milk, the saddler made a leather collar, fitted with sharp iron spikes; these pricked the tender skin of the cow when the calf tried to suckle. Self-suckling was (as we have seen) an undesirable habit of some cows; fitted with a larger version of the weaning collar, they were soon cured of this tendency.

The saddler co-operated with other craftsmen, for example in the manufacture of the leather parts for the carriage or cart made by the wheelwright. In one Suffolk village, where the wheelwright's shop faced the saddlery across the street, the wheelwright would say, 'You make me a set of harness, and I'll make you a cart'. Any difference would be adjusted later.

Changes in the way of life, especially in the country, have been reflected in the effect on the saddler's work. More and more the tendency has been for concentration in the towns, and in the absorption of the small craftsman into the firms covering the whole field of work. As in the case of the farrier, an increase in the number of people taking up riding as a form of exercise has maintained the demand for riding equipment, but mechanization on the farm, and on the road, have lessened the need for the services of the village saddler, at least. It will be interesting to see to what extent the reversal of the trend, due to the huge rise in the cost of sources of energy, which has already resulted in some degree of return to the use of the horse on the land, will restore the place of the saddler in the local economy.

8 *The Saddler's Tools*
　　1. Clamp　2. Head-knife　3. Half-moon knife　4. Gauge　5, 6. Edge-tools
　　7. Hand-iron　8. Stitch-punch (15 stitches to the inch)　9. Stitch-punch
　　(7 stitches to the inch)　10. Palm-iron　11. Prick-wheel, roulette
　　12. Creasing-iron (quadruple)　13. Creaser, marker　14. Punch
　　15. Creasing-iron (double, adjustable)　(No. 1: 1/8; 4: 1/6;
　　remainder 1/3)

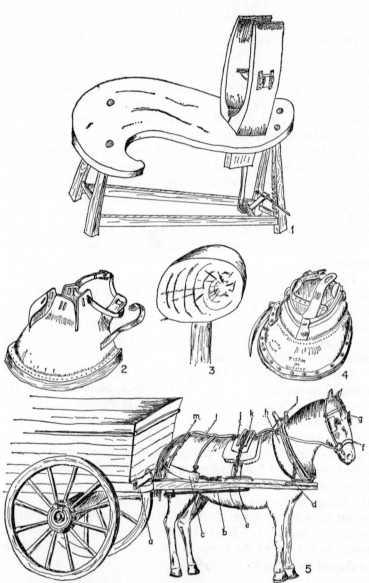

9 *The Saddler's Equipment and Products*
   1. Saddler's stool   2, 4. Horse-boots, lawn-boots   3. Collar-mallet
   5. Horse with tumbril (*a*. toe-bar; *b*. shaft-stay; *c*. breeching, with chain
   and hook; *d*. tug-chain connecting tug-hooks on hames and shafts;
   e. girth; *f*. bridle, *dutfin*; *g*. blinkers, *winkers*; *h*. collar; *i*. hames, *seals*,
   secured by housing-strap; *j*. cart-saddle; *k*. ridge-chain; *l*. back-strap or
   meeter-strap, with hip-straps to breechings; *m*. crupper, passing under
   tail (No. 1 : 1/12; 2, 3 and 4 : 1/6)

As in a number of crafts, the saddler employs devices to ensure firm control of his material, whilst leaving his hands as free as possible to manipulate his tools; the clamp consists of two lengths of oak or ash, about three feet six inches in length and two to three inches in width, firmly joined at the base, and curving outward, then inward, to meet at the top, where they are bevelled to form a grip, strongly reminiscent of a pair of tweezers. The saddler sits with the clamp gripped between the knees, and it in turn grips the leather. The saddler's stool is really a variant of the clamp, providing a seat for the worker as well as teeth which can be held in position by an adjustable bar, which latches on to one of a series of studs.

Just as the tailor or dressmaker cuts material with as great economy as possible to fit the pattern, so does the saddler, but he must take account of a further factor. Leather varies in thickness, and cutting must allow for the strongest part to coincide with that area of the article to be made which will be subject to the greatest wear.

The knives used for cutting leather are peculiar to the craft, and bear no resemblance to those used in any other work. The most characteristic and unusual is the *half-moon* knife, also known as the *round-knife*. The blade is semicircular or crescentic in shape, and set transversely on the short, stocky handle. The blade may measure as much as six inches across, and about two and a half inches in length. Other variants have a blade of rather more triangular form, or *half-round*, projecting more to one side than the other. These knives are used in several ways, for cutting and paring down where leather is to be spliced.

A hand-knife of the kind used in many crafts is needed for the usual small jobs of cutting off the odd piece, or severing twine, etc.

Edge-tools somewhat resemble a fork, with a blade set between the prongs. They are used for trimming off the sharp edge left when the leather has been cut, and for bevelling. Nomenclature varies, even within the same county; one saddler discriminated between the edge-tool with a long, fine blade, and one with a broader blade, which he called a *skiver*, a name which he also applied to the small *plough* used for cutting straps to the required width. Normally, the term *skiver* is taken to mean the fine layer of leather cut off from a sheepskin for such tasks as bookbinding, etc., or the tool for paring off this. Yet another used the term *edging tools*.

Then there are the tools variously called *veins*, *creasers* or *creasing-irons*. These have a lozenge-shaped head, and are used for marking leather; a creaser is used to indent the lines which run just inside the margin of a strap; it is heated before use as a general rule. There are single-headed creasers, a double creaser with two parallel blades, and one in which these blades are adjustable as to width by means of a screw. A shouldered creaser allows more pressure to be brought to bear.

In order to ensure even stitchery, the leather is first marked with a *stitch-punch*, a short punch with a flat, blade-like head, with short teeth, varying in number according to the length of stitch intended. A *prick-wheel* or *stitch-wheel* performs a similar function. It is often made to take interchangeable heads with teeth ranging from a separation of one-eighth of an inch to very fine.

Punches of various sizes and shapes are used for cutting the holes in straps.

When the position has been marked for the holes, the leather is pierced with an *awl* of suitable size, according to the nature of the work. Needles, too, must be of different grades, and are helped on their way through the leather by means of a *hand-iron*, a tool superficially resembling a creasing-iron, but with the tip circular, and bent over at an angle. In the centre of the tip is a small pit which accommodates the head of the needle. In collar-making, the *palm-iron* is used for this purpose. It has a hollow, pear-shaped body, fitting the palm of the hand. The inner surface is pitted to give a purchase on the needle. From the narrow, forward end of the iron projects a neck towards the tip of which is a lozenge-shaped hole which may be used to grip the needle after its passage through the leather and pull it through.

Other tools are best described in discussing the processes which they serve.

The object of the saddle is not merely to give the rider a comfortable seat; it is also designed to ease the burden for the horse by supporting the weight of the rider in such a way as to prevent undue pressure on the horse's backbone. Essentially, then, the saddle consists of an arched frame, the saddle-tree, consisting of two side-bars, resting on either side of the backbone, and supporting two arches, one in front and one behind, raised sufficiently to ensure that the actual frame does not come in contact with the backbone. The saddle-tree was formerly made of beechwood, but is now more usually of steel or other metal. Webbing, applied wet in order that it may become taut on drying, is then stretched over the saddle-tree, followed by layers of cloth, traditionally linen and serge, now sometimes replaced by synthetic fabrics, though serge is still mostly used; wool is stuffed into the space between the two layers, using the *seat-iron*, a handled tool with a flat blade some fourteen inches in length, by half an inch wide. The tip is flexible, to prevent damage to the fabric when stuffing.

Although the saddler gets his name from the fact that he makes saddles, the task calling for the greatest skill is collar-making. Whereas the saddle is made to fit a particular type of horse, and can be transferred within limits from one horse to another, the collar is made for the individual horse, after careful measurements have been taken. It has been stated that it was this individuality of the collar which caused its use to be discontinued for military purposes and for the substitution of breast-harness.* Particularly in the case of the artillery, the losses of horses in battle posed a serious problem when the collar could not be transferred from one horse to another.

Making starts with the *wale*, the roll to which the body of the collar is attached, and which forms a housing for the *hames* (*sails* in Suffolk) which give attachment for the shafts of the vehicle to be pulled, or to the traces. It is made from a strong, tough variety of leather. Exact measurement is essential before the wale is made up, as the correct fitting of the collar will depend on the accuracy with which the wale is made. The collar must be a perfect fit, as through it the horse will take the full strain of the pull.

A strip of leather, rather longer than the double length of the collar, is doubled over and stitched to form a roll, leaving the edges projecting sufficiently to allow of the body of the collar to be joined on to the wale. The wale is stuffed with rye straw, used because of its fine texture, lacking the knots formed by the nodes of the straw, which are more prominent in wheat straw. In the event of rye straw being unobtainable, it was on occasion necessary to resort to wheat, but this had to be of good quality, and the saddler would apply to a farmer who had grown the older variety of long-straw wheat for thatching. The saddler would go and pull out straw from the stack, so as to be able to select the best, but even this was never used if rye straw could be got.

* G. Tylden, *Discovering Harness and Saddlery*, Shire Publications, 1971, p. 10.

The tool used for the purpose is the *collar-stuffing iron*, somewhat resembling the *seat-iron* used for the same task in the making of a saddle, but entirely of iron, seventeen inches in length, of round section but flattening to a blade with a forked tip; the butt ended in a circular button, one inch in diameter. A few straws are caught up in the fork, and pushed down into the wale; the next wisp will fit into the 'V' thus formed, and so on until stuffing is complete. A slightly curved iron is used to get right down into the base of the wale, in which is a *pipe iron* curved to ensure a well-shaped end. In order to force the straw well in, the collar is reversed at intervals striking the butt on the ground. This iron is also sometimes used for saddle-stuffing.

The body of the collar is padded with wool, and stuffed with straw, and if it is intended for draught work, is lined with the traditional checked collar flannel.

For a horse liable to sore shoulders, a collar is sometimes made entirely of rush, or more usually of sedge. This led to an interesting practice followed by a Suffolk saddler. He did not make collars for other than draught horses as a rule, but kept a stock of sedge collars of various sizes suitable for what he described as 'trap-horses'. When a farmer ordered a new set of harness for his cob or pony, a sedge collar was first fitted, and would be worn by the horse during the time that the harness was in process of making. By the time this was nearly ready, the collar would have become well moulded to the animal. It was then covered with leather, and the whole set of harness was complete.

The loop by which the blinker or *winker* is attached to the bridle calls for another tool especially for the purpose, the *loop-stick*, which may be either of wood or iron. A hot *creasing-iron* is used for the decoration on the loop.

Although the village saddler was likely to be more concerned with the making of draught harness for use on the farm than with riding equipment, or the light harness for use with passenger vehicles, this work called for the same degree of skill and accuracy in its fabrication as the more elegant carriage type. Rough and sturdy in appearance though it might be, it must provide the same measure of comfort for the animal. The cumbrous breechings must fit snugly over the hind-parts; the collar has to take a considerable strain, and this and the pad-saddle must not rub or chafe. The latter is often padded with the same quality of flannel as that used

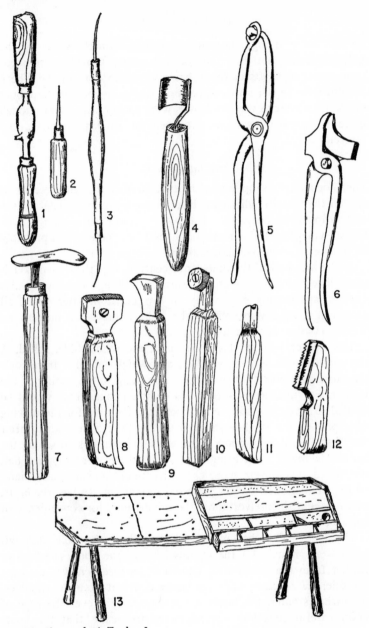

10 *The Shoe-maker's Tools – I*
1. Glazer, long-stick 2. Stab-awl 3. Awl 4. Drag-knife 5. Stretching-
pliers 6. Lasting-pincers 7. Knee-last, hobbing-foot, *punion* 8. Seat-
healer, seat-iron 9. Burnisher, glazing-iron 10. Slide box-wheel, wheel-
iron, *fudge-wheel* 11. Waist-iron 12. Roughing-tool 13. Cobbler's stool
(All 1/3, except 1 : 1/6; 7 : 1/18; 13 : 1/12)

for the collar lining. The saddle-tree was formerly made by the saddler himself, but the *hames* or *seals* which provide attachment from collar to shafts or trace-chains were the work of the wheel-wright, who kept a series of patterns just as he did for the felloes of the wheels. Such wooden hames were usual on the farm, though more spectacular examples are seen on carriage harness, and brewer's drays.

THE SHOE-MAKER

The shoe-maker's shop was as much a part of the village scene as that of the wheelwright or the blacksmith; more so, perhaps, as the early directories frequently list two or more to a village. One Suffolk village had nine in 1930, but most of these would probably be repairers rather than shoe-makers.

In the first half of the nineteenth century, too, the shoe-maker is often listed as 'shoe-maker and currier', although there were also curriers specializing exclusively in this craft. In later years, all processes necessary to render the hide suitable for making up were performed at the tannery.

The leather was purchased in *butts*, the whole hide, rolled. A roll might measure some six feet, and weigh anything from four-teen to eighteen or twenty pounds, according to the quality of the leather. For instance, a sixteen- to eighteen-pound butt would be needed to give the quality and dimensions required for the making of a pair of the thigh-boots used by the fishermen. Shortly after the First World War, about 1920, the tanneries took to selling the leather in *bends*, each being a half-butt; these were supplied flat, not rolled. They were more expensive than the *butts*, and many of the smaller shoe-makers preferred to continue to buy the *butts*, cutting them themselves down the middle line, for convenience of storage.

The hide had to be cut as economically as possible; different parts were suitable for the various parts of the boot. The heavier leather from the spinal area, known as *butt-leather*, was used for the sole; *belly-leather* made the insole, and that from the shoulder, somewhat stouter, the insole for sea-boots. Whatever the type of boot, careful selection was necessary to ensure that the boots would match in every respect, so that they were comfortable, and wore evenly.

As in other crafts, there was some degree of specialization

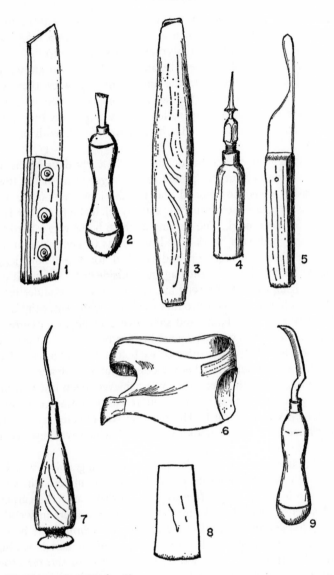

11 *The Shoe-maker's Tools – II*
1. Hack-knife   2. Welt-pricker   3. Welt-rubber   4. Peg-awl   5. Clicking-knife   6. Hand-leather   7. Curved awl   8. Scraper   9. Seat-file   (All 1/3)

depending on the particular requirements of the locality. In the rural areas, a stout boot known as the *high-low* (often rendered as 'hillow' in the records and accounts), was made for the farm-worker. It came well up over the ankle, and was also known as a *fourteen-holer*, a reference to the number of lace-holes; these were generally merely pierced with the awl, and not fitted with brass eyelets; the sole was heavily nailed to give a grip on the slippery mud. A later boot was the *Blucher*, of lower cut, with only five lace-holes.

Some riding boots were made, but by the early days of this century this trade had largely passed to the larger firms in the towns.

In coastal areas the demand was for the long *thigh-boots* worn by the fishermen. These must be entirely of leather; rubber is too slippery for deck-work. The making of these boots was a hard task, taking two good days' work. The leather was turned inside out, the two edges brought together, and stitched for the whole length. Then the boot had to be turned again – outside out – a difficult exercise, requiring the aid of strong pincers. The use of shoulder leather for the insole helped to ensure that the boots were water-tight.

As a general rule, boots and shoes were made to measure, not for stock. Lasts for every size were kept in readiness, and provision was made for the peculiarities of each foot by adding small cuts of leather to the surface where necessary, and sandpapering these down until a smooth, even finish was achieved. Each last was made in two parts, so that it could be more easily extracted from the shoe which was built on it. The removal was effected by means of the *last-hook*, an angled hook the point of which was inserted in a hole in the last.

A characteristic of the craftsman is the ingenuity which he displays in devising a means of controlling his material in such a way as to leave his hands free to perform their task. The carpenter has his bench vice, the rake-maker and other workers in wood the *shaving-horse* and the *brake*, the saddler his *clamp* held between the knees. The *clamp* is also used by the shoe-maker; it is almost identical with that of the saddler, but generally of shorter, stouter build, as the cobbler's stool is low. Another device, used more for repair work than actual shoe-making, is the *knee-last*, *hobbing-foot* or *punion*, a stout post of round section, with a socket in the head, into which lasts of various sizes can be fitted.

The thread used for stitching is now largely nylon, but until

I Roman numerals used to facilitate the assembly of a timber-framed building; the cart-lodge of the Alton watermill.

II The saw-pit at Blaxhall, Suffolk; the 'tiller' handle is fixed on the saw; the pitman is holding the box-handle to be attached to the lower end.

III   The 'timber-jim' used by H. W. Baldry, wheelwright, of Horham; note the straked wheels.

IV   A 'hermaphrodite' wagon; the tumbril could be used separately; attachment of the fore-carriage converted it to a harvest-wagon.

V   The smithy of Charles Clouting, of Boyton.

VI   'Shoeing' a wheel; the heated tyre is placed on the wheel, which is
      secured to the 'plate'.

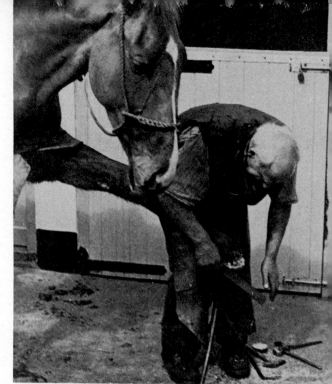

VII Filing down the clenched nails; Hector Moore of Brandeston using the tripod to support the hoof.

VIII The Saddler at work; A. G. Pearson, of Washbrook, stitching on the flannel lining of a cart-saddle.

IX Brian Palfrey, cooper, 'raising' a cask, using mallet and driver.

X   Using the croze to form the groove which takes the head of the cask.

XI   *Above* Cutting reed for thatching on the marshes at Walberswick.

XII   *Right* George John thatching a cottage with straw; driving in a broatch with the mallet.

XIII *Below* Thatching a house with reed, at Ovington, Essex; Frank Linnett using the leggatt to beat in the reed; on the right is a gable with thatching complete; barges and eaves cut; ridge thatched with straw, secured with liggers.

XIV The rake-maker's steam-box; both rake-stails and scythe-sneads are steamed to render them pliable.

XV Noël Cullum using the stail-engine; at Welnetham the stail is revolved and the engine simply pushed forward.

XVI *Right* Frank Bird
    'ironing' a beetle; the
    heated rings are
    beaten on, using the
    handled ring and bar.
XVII *Below* Making a
    gate-hurdle.

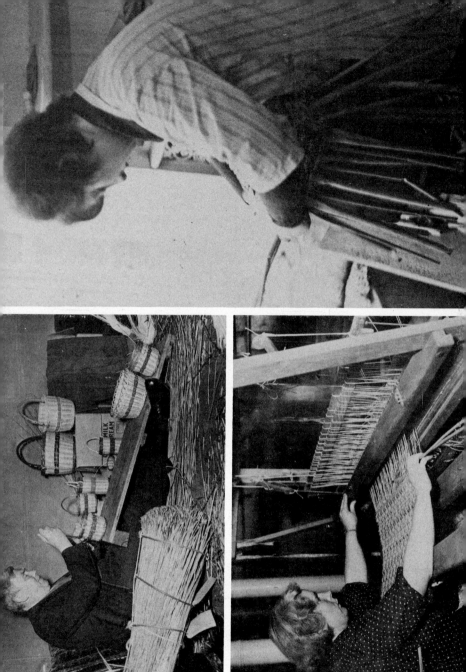

XVIII Victor Carman, a blind basket-maker, using the lap-board.

XIX   Making a basket of rushes.

XX   Weaving rushes on the loom at Debenham.

XXI   *Opposite, top* Cutting rushes for the Deben rush-weavers.

XXII   *Opposite, bottom* Norfolk rush-cutters with a laden marsh-boat.

XXIII *Above* Stacking 'green' bricks to ripen; the process has not varied since this photograph was taken at Tuddenham, *c.* 1900.

XXIV   *Below* Drying sheds at the Cove bottom Brickworks, 1976.

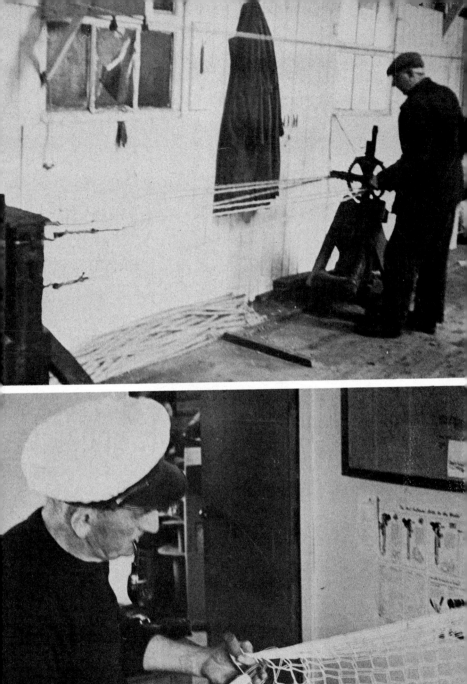

XXIX *Right* Norton Field hanging baulks of herrings on racks in the smoke-house, for 'kippering'; quite an acrobatic feat.

XXX *Below* Slotting whole herring on to rods, which are then hung on racks to be placed in the smoke-house; they will emerge as bloaters.

XXXI *Opposite, top* Leonard Calver making cider in a traditional press.

XXXII *Opposite, bottom* A dairying class at West Row, *c.* 1903; these classes were arranged jointly by the Suffolk and Norfolk County Councils.

XXXIII   *Above* A traditional post-mill, before the days of the round-house; Markham's Mill, Snape.

XXXIV   *Above, right* The fantail of the post-mill at Holton St Peter; it brought the buck round into the wind.

XXXV   *Below* Billingford tower windmill, Norfolk.

XXXVI   *Below, right* The Herringfleet wind-pump; of smock-hill construction; many others were tower mills, of brick.

recently was always prepared by the shoe-maker himself. Hempen fibres, the thickness varying according to the task in hand, were twisted together using *cobbler's wax* prepared by boiling pitch mixed with neat's-foot oil. At either end of each length of thread a pig's bristle was inserted to assist the introduction of the thread into the hole made by an awl, and its passage through the leather. During the process of stitching a harder wax, prepared from the pitch but without the addition of oil, was used to lubricate the thread.

The uppers of the shoe were cut from *belly-leather*, or *kip-leather* (of lighter quality, between a calf and a cow-hide). Calf and kid were also used. Cutting was done with a long, slender-bladed knife, the *clicking-knife*, and the sections were then stitched together, the holes being first pierced with the *stab-awl*. The thread had to be drawn tight, and this could be hard on the hands; the shoe-maker therefore wore on his left hand a *hand-leather*, a kind of mitten without fingers, and with a hole for the thumb. A well-worn hand-leather is deeply scored where the thread has cut into it, with here and there patches at the more vulnerable points.

When the uppers are ready, they are fitted on the last, and drawn tightly over it with the *lasting-pincers*.

The leather for the sole is soaked, and well beaten with a hammer on the *lap-stone*. This was originally a flat stone, but frequently its place was taken by an ordinary flat-iron, the handle of which had first been removed.

Sole and heel were made up of layers, the inner of belly-leather, the outer of butt-leather. The leather for the *welt* was subject to special preparation at the tannery, where it was impregnated with a mixture of oil and wax. Some makers bought the leather in strips, others ready-made welts.

When the insole had been secured in place, the sole was attached with wooden pegs driven into holes made with the *peg-awl*, which had an adjustable socket like that of a brace, into which could be fitted bits of different size.

The heel was similarly attached, the ends of the pegs projecting inside the shoe, where they were subsequently shaved off with the *drag-knife*.

Any rough surfaces were smoothed with the *scraper*, a metal plate with a sharp edge. In former times a fragment of broken glass served the same purpose.

The *welt* was the subject of particular attention, for on its quality depended the effective waterproofing of the shoe. It was pressed in with the *welt-rubber*, a smooth flattened implement of oval section, tapering to the ends at each of which was a ridge, differing in thickness, which was applied in the channel between welt and upper. Each stitch was pressed in with the *welt-pricker*, and the *seat-file* used to open up the channel. Then the *slide box-wheel*, *wheel-iron* or *fudge-wheel* was run round the welt to mark it.

The *double-iron*, heated, spread the heel-ball round the edge of the sole, and the *waist-iron*, also applied hot, ensured that the wax reached over the edge of the sole. *Heel-ball* was applied to the heel with the *burnisher* or *glazing-iron*, and the underside of the sole polished with the *glazer*, also known as the *long-stick*, for with the rounded end of the handle it is possible to smooth out any inequalities in, for instance, the inside of a riding-boot.

Pressure on a deformity such as a bunion can be relieved by the use of the *stretching-pliers*.

The shoe-maker's rasp dispenses with a handle, providing four different grades of surface by using both ends and both sides of the implement.

A heavy knife, the *hack-knife*, with a stout blade, performs much the same function in this craft as the farrier's *buffer*; it is used for removing toe-plates, heel-irons and *hobs*, when repairing heavy boots such as highlows.

A century ago a serviceable and presentable pair of boots, made to measure, could be had for about twelve shillings and sixpence, or a little over sixty pence in the new currency. At the present day, a pair bought 'off the shelf' might be had for fifteen or twenty pounds.

V
The Cooper

As in the case of so many craftsmen, the cooper, once an indispensable member of the rural community, has seen the demand for his wares diminish with the increase in the production of factory-made utensils. Where he was 'self-employed' he served an area rather than a village, and was often itinerant; sometimes he was employed by a brewery, or aboard ship, where the cask was found to be the most convenient method of transporting much of the cargo, as well as the ship's stores.* Regrettably the brewer's cask has now been largely replaced by the ugly metal barrel. Can beer so stored taste the same? It is, in fact, only about two years since the brewery of Greene, King and Company, at Bury St Edmunds, ceased to employ a cooper.†

In the simple economy of the countryside, the cooper had an important part to play. For the farm, he made the wooden pails for carrying water from the well, and the milk from the cow-shed. In earlier times, the churn for butter-making had a simple barrel form, and was the work of the cooper, though it soon passed to the specialized province of the factory, as new fittings were developed. The shallow keeler, in which the butter was washed, was cooper-made, and a similar vessel was used in home brewing, for which he also supplied casks for storage, and the smaller barrels taken to the harvest field to slake the thirst of the reapers.

* Geraint Jenkins, in his *Traditional Country Craftsmen*, 1965, relates how the Coopers' Company, apparently in existence since 1298 but chartered in 1501, employed a beadle to counter such practices as the making of casks by coopers employed by the brewers; this was illegal until the eighteenth century.
† Brian Palfrey, who succeeded his father in the post. (See my *Life and Tradition in Suffolk and North-East Essex*, 1976).

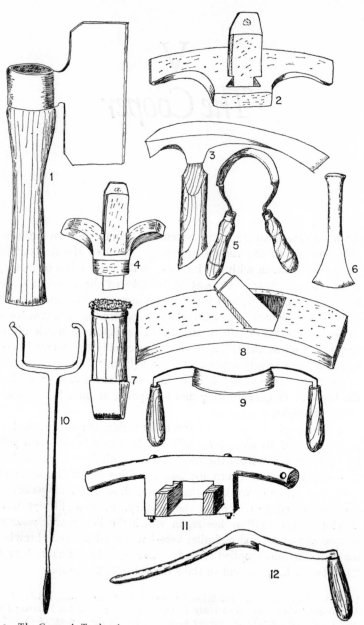

The Cooper's Tools – 1
1. Broad-axe   2. Downright-shave   3. Rending-adze   4. Inside-shave
5. Two-handed shave, round shave   6. Chintzing-iron   7. Driver   8. Sun-
plane   9. Hollowing-knife   10. Flagging-iron   11. Buzz   12. Jigger
(All 1/6)

The tools of the cooper rival in number and variety those of the wheelwright; indeed, a comparison readily springs to mind as one watches the cooper at work shaping the staves of a cask with his *broad-axe*. Like that of the wheelwright, it is used rather for *planing* than chopping, and like that implement, too, it is bevelled on only one side.

The wood for the staves is sawn into suitable lengths, and split with a *froe* similar to that of the wheelwright; they are then smoothed with a draw-knife, and tapered to give the necessary bowed shape, wider at the centre than the top and bottom, with the broad-axe. Next, the sides must be bevelled so that when the cask is assembled they will knit snugly together; this is done on the *jointer-plane*, often six feet or so in length, and thus incapable of manipulation in the ordinary way; it is mounted on feet, resting at an angle, and the stave is drawn across the blade.

The next stage is known as *raising* the cask. The prepared staves are assembled in a complete circle, held in place by an iron *raising hoop* at the top. In order to prevent the staves from falling apart, a *truss hoop*, made of ash, a resilient wood, is driven down over them; this is not made by the cooper, somewhat strangely, but is supplied to him by the hurdle-maker or other worker in wood. Additional iron hoops are now placed in position, driven on by means of a short iron-shod *driver* and hammer. At this stage the distal ends are still splayed out. The staves are next wetted and steamed over a *cresset*, a small basket fire, and forced together with the aid of more ash hoops, a process known as trussing. The firing of the cresset provides the occasion for combining neatness with economy; the shaving formed in preparing the staves serve as fuel. A further spell of heating dries the cask and ensures its stability.

Now comes the process of topping, and once again, as in the case of the axe, the skill of the craftsman achieves a result which seems out of all proportion to the seemingly crude form of the tool employed, a short-handled adze with strongly curved blade. With this the circumference of the top is pared to form the *chime*, the inner bevel of the top of the cask. The top is next planed level with the *sun-plane*, which is curved to follow the circular form.

The interior of the cask must now be smoothed down with the *jigger*, a specialized draw-knife with one handle of wood, at right angles to the blade, and a steel grip in the same plane as the blade, which is short and strongly curved. The cask is now ready for the

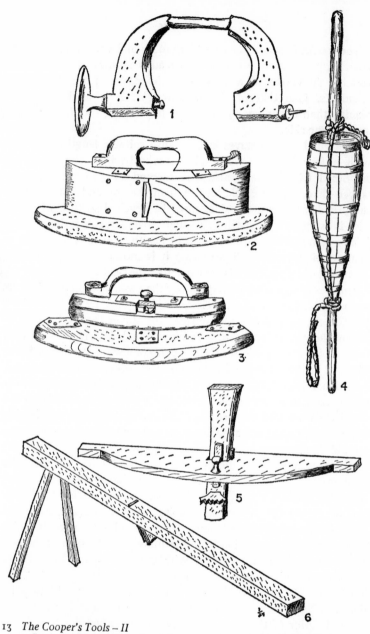

13 *The Cooper's Tools – II*
   1. Brace, with extra large head, for use against breast   2. Chiv, chive
   3. Croze   4. Marker-buoy (cooper-made)   5. Croze (a very early type)
   6. Jointer-plane (2 & 3 were used by a boat-builder)   (No. 4: 1/18;
   6: 1/12; remainder 1/6)

cutting of the *howel*, a groove of semicircular form cut round the inside of the cask a little way below the chime by means of the *chiv* or *chive*, a kind of plane with a semicircular surface corresponding with the shape of the interior of the top. A similiar plane, but with a much narrower blade, the *croze*, is used to cut the groove into the howel to take the head. Any irregularities of the inside are removed with the *inside-shave* and *round-shave*.

The radius of the head is calculated by stepping a compass round the top of the cask, adjusting it until a measurement of one-sixth of the perimeter is found. The head is rounded with the *heading swift*, a large draw-knife.

A small iron chisel, not unlike a cold chisel but with a broader blade, the *chintzing-iron*, is used to force pieces of dried rush into the joint where the head fits into the groove made with the croze, and indeed any other joints liable to allow leakage, as for instance the pieces of which the head is made. Where similar caulking is required between the staves, a tool with forked head, the *flagging-iron*, is employed to force the staves apart; its distal end has a flattened spoon-shaped tip for packing in the rushes.

The exterior of the cask is smoothed off with the *buzz*, a specialized form of draw-shave, and the *downright-shave*.

There appears to be less local variation in the tools used by the cooper than in some of the other crafts, but in East Anglia the *shaving-horse*, in common use elsewhere, seems to be seldom employed, except for the making of the smaller casks and milk pails. The *jigger*, here used as already indicated for the final smoothing of the interior, is said by Jenkins (*op. cit.*) to be used in repair work for cutting the channel for the head.

The bung-hole of the cask is bored with the *taper-auger*, but the *thief*, for trimming the hole after boring, seems not to be used here.

As was the case with other crafts, the cooper's work was affected by the needs of the area in which he worked. As in the countryside he catered for the farmer, and the farmer's wife, and perhaps made a *gotch* to satisfy the thirst of the bell-ringers in the village church, so by the sea he made barrels for the herring fishers, and even the marker-buoys which had to withstand the force of the gales at sea.

VI
The Thatcher

Where houses be reeded (as houses have need),
Now pare off the moss, and go beat in the reed:
Five Hundred Points of Good Husbandry, THOMAS TUSSER, 1571

Just as the principal building material in early times was timber in its natural state, so the means of giving protection from the elements was ready to hand in other forms of vegetation. In tropical countries, it was usually the leaves of the palms, with their spreading fronds; in areas of moorland – heather; in our countryside generally, the straw produced by the growing of cereal crops, or the reeds with which our marshes abound.

Both straw and reed are well adapted for such a use; their stems consist of hollow cylinders which hold the air, forming an ideal insulating layer, in something of the same manner as the feathers of the birds which, on a cold day, may be seen fluffed out to enclose as great a volume of air as possible (or, for that matter, the string vest favoured by explorers in cold regions).

Thatch is thus capable of keeping out both the cold of winter and the excessive heat of summer. It is light in weight, resistant to rain, and surprisingly durable. Generally speaking, and of course subject to local conditions, one may think in terms of a life of thirty years or even more for straw (a house at Denston in Suffolk, thatched with reed in 1973, had been straw-thatched by the same thatcher's father forty-five years before), and sixty to as much as a hundred for reed. Thatch has two disadvantages: it attracts small birds seeking a convenient nesting-place, and it is regarded as a high fire risk by some insurance companies. Fine wire-netting will discourage the birds, and there are means of rendering thatch, if not fire-proof, at least fire-resistant.

By a strange quirk of fate, the craft owes its survival in very great degree to the fact that the buildings for which it provides protection are largely no longer in the occupation of those for whom they were originally intended, but have been bought up by those who have succumbed to the fascination of the picturesque, and can afford the costly business of replacing worn thatch, something beyond the means of the cottager or the small farmer, who have tended to substitute tiles or slates, or even that abomination, if adequate protection, corrugated iron or asbestos sheeting.

In these conditions the craft is actually flourishing; although numbers have naturally declined by some seventy or eighty per cent in the last hundred years, those remaining have their order books full for years to come. Sadly, some have descended to the use of a simulated thatch of plastic.

Both straw and reed are ideally suited for the thatcher's work, not only by their nature, but because both are readily available, and quick-growing. The proportions in which they are used, however, have changed greatly in recent years. In former times, straw thatch was most common; it was cheaper, and obtainable after every harvest throughout the region; reed grew only where marshy conditions prevailed. All this has been changed by mechanization on the farms. No longer is straw needed for fodder and bedding for the horses which have virtually disappeared from the farm; it is generally regarded as a nuisance, to be got rid of as soon as possible, often by burning to the detriment of the hedgerows and the wild life which finds a home there. Only recently, and to a limited extent, has there been a demand for supplies from East Anglia for the farmers of the south-west. A short-strawed variety of wheat is better suited for reaping with the combine-harvester. The straw is not only too short for the thatcher's purpose, but the stems are crushed and mangled, destroying their insulating properties. Even the reed-thatcher needs straw for the ridges; reed is not sufficiently pliable. The thatcher must therefore make an arrangement with a farmer to grow a proportion of long-straw wheat, to reap it with a 'binder' or sail-reaper, and to thresh it with the drum. The practice varies; one thatcher finds a farmer willing to carry out all

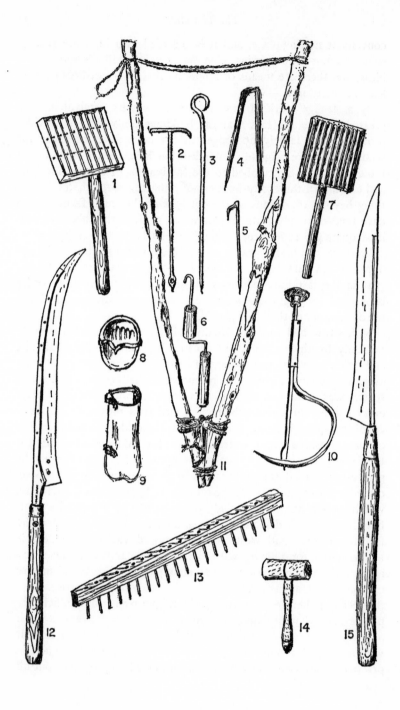

these processes; he says that it is usually the older farmers who are equipped to do this, as might be expected, and quoted Attleborough, in Norfolk, as a good source for the right quality of straw, though he is a Suffolk thatcher. Another will arrange for the farmer to grow the crop, but will both cut and thresh it himself, and yet another rents a field, sowing, reaping and threshing his own crop. It has been said that some of the farmers supplying straw to the thatchers get more for the straw than for the grain.

Two thatchers, working widely apart, one in the north of Suffolk and the other on the borders of Suffolk and Essex, both have high praise for rye as material for ridging. It is soft to the hands, and pliable, but tough in wear.

Reed (*Phragmites communis*) is usually known as 'Norfolk Reed', and perhaps a major source is the Ranworth Broad in Norfolk, but it also grows extensively on the marshes round Walberswick in Suffolk. Some is still cut by hand, but most is now machine-cut, the thatcher employing a contractor, in one case, at least, from as far away as Dorset. The reed-beds are on land in private ownership, and payment is made to the landowner according to quantity.

Whichever material is used, it must first be tied into bundles of convenient size. The straw is gathered together by means of a straw-buncher, a hook with a blade of rounded section, curved to enclose a bundle of about one foot in diameter, known as a yelm (yealm), gavel or 'gabble'. The term yelm is often loosely applied to reed as well as straw, but should strictly be used only for the latter. The Norfolk word for a bundle of reed is a bolt; a Suffolk thatcher, when asked. 'What do you call these bundles?' replied simply, 'Well – bundles!' When reed is harvested by hand, the size of the bundle is so calculated that five or so together will have a girth of six feet – a fathom – but the term is hardly ever used now that machine cutting is the general rule.

Whether using straw or reed, the thatcher must have in readiness a number of artifacts needed for placing the thatch in position, and securing it in place. The term used by a Suffolk thatcher for these was 'spicks'; more usually they are referred to as *thatching-*

14 *The Thatcher's Tools*
   1. Leggatt (modern, of steel) 2, 3. Needles 4. Broatch, *brawtch*
   5. Thatch-pin 6. Scud-winder, throw-crook 7. Leggatt (old, wooden)
   8. Knee-pad (modern, of rubber) 9. Knee-pad (old, of leather) 10. Stack-
   thatching needle 11. Yoke 12. Eaves-knife 13. Rake 14. Mallet
   15. Flue-knife, barge-knife (All 1/12)

spars. Of these, *sways* are rods of split hazel (or sometimes willow), which are pinned down to the rafters by means of iron *thatch-pins* to hold firm the rows of yealms or bolts; *liggers* are shorter rods arranged in a criss-cross pattern to secure the straw ridge, and are held down by yet another form of spar, the *broatch* (*brawtch*), a short hazel spar, which by a deft twist is converted into a staple. It was at one time customary for the spars to be made by a specialist, or by one of the regular craftsmen in wood, such as the hurdle-maker, but they are now frequently made by the thatcher himself. There may be two good reasons for this; Cyril Rackham, who comes from a line of thatchers dating back for four hundred years, and hails from Bramfield, much prefers to leave the making of spars to others, but finds it increasingly difficult to find a maker, so has to fall back on his own efforts from time to time. When this is the case, he cuts his own coppiced hazel, 'when they'll let you go into the woods' – pheasant-rearing makes owners increasingly unwilling to allow this. Frank Linnett, whose thatching forbears can be traced back for a mere three hundred years, and who works at the other side of the county, on the Essex borders, prefers to make his own spars and broatches during the long winter evenings. Behind his house are neat stacks of spars and broatches, and in his own small forge he hammers out the iron thatch-pins. The *spar-hook*, a small bill-hook, is used for splitting the hazel wands, often into as many as six sections.

For work requiring great skill, the equipment is surprisingly simple and the tools few. Clambering about on ladders on a sloping roof calls for some protection for the knees. *Knee-pads* were formerly of leather, and were as often as not made by the thatcher; they are now factory-made, of foam rubber. For carrying the yealms or bolts up the ladder to the roof the *yoke*, a forked branch of hazel or some similiar wood is used. If a natural fork can be cut, so much the better, but more often it is necessary to join two lengths of four or five feet to form a 'V', held in position by a wooden block, the tips of the arms notched and linked by a length of twine.

Three main methods of thatching are used; reed is now the most common. The *bolts* or bundles are laid in overlapping series beginning at the eaves, each row held in position by *sways*, and secured to the underlying rafters by *thatch-pins*; the cut ends thus project at the surface, and are beaten in to give a tight, uniform cover with the *leggatt*, traditionally a wooden bat with a rectangular or rounded head. For reed-thatching, the surface may be pierced with holes, or studded with nails. A modern development has a rectangular head of steel, divided by cross-walls into square compartments.

For *straw-reed*-thatching, the *leggatt* has a series of longitudinal grooves. Long-straw wheat is specially grown for this purpose, cut with sail-reaper or binder, and threshed with a *drum* equipped with an attachment which combs the wheat so that all the heads face the same way.

In *long-straw*-thatching, the *yealms* are laid in a similar manner, but are not beaten with the *leggatt* but combed with the side-rake, resulting in a fine, flowing surface, which glistens in the sun. The rake is often made by the simple expedient of driving in nails at intervals in a length of wood, but a fine example in the Museum of East Anglian Life has a shaft of untrimmed ash, with twelve tines of hazel – in itself an example of superb craftsmanship.

Whether reed or straw, the ends at the eaves are trimmed with the *eaves-knife*, a long-handled knife the blade of which may be have been made from an old scythe-blade. The gables or *barges* are similarly trimmed with the *flue-knife*. This resembles the eaves-knife, but the curve of the blade is backward, not forward, at least in the example available. So frequently the form of the tool was determined by the availability of material. The modern reed-thatcher often uses steel rods in place of sways. In telling of this, Cyril Rackham added, 'They're terribly expensive!' – seeming to reflect an unconscious dislike, encountered on more than one occasion in men of various crafts, of the fact that craftsmanship is subject to the same inflationary pressures as the rest of the economy.

When the bolt of reed is placed in position, it may be held temporarily by inserting a *needle*, an iron rod, varying in length, with a flattened leaf-shaped point in which is an eye. The needle, however, has another use, in which the eye plays an essential role. If the thatch is to be tied to the rafters, one end of a length of tarred twine is tied to the sway or ligger, and the other threaded through the eye of the needle, which is then pushed through the thatch to an assistant inside the roof. He detaches the twine, passes it round the rafter, and secures it once more to the needle, which is then drawn back to the surface, and the twine attached again to the sway.

Reed is more durable than straw, but is too tough and unyielding for use for the ridge or coping. For this, straw is used, and as has already been noted, rye straw is preferred by many thatchers because of its softness in handling – soft yet tough and weather-resistant. Moreover, rye is usually still grown with a long stalk, and is therefore ideal. The straw is laid over the ridge, and held in position with liggers laid cross-wise, and fixed with broatches of hazel, driven home with a beechwood mallet. The edges of the coping are trimmed into patterns sometimes said to have a regional significance, but more frequently expressing the taste of the thatcher.

In the days when the harvested corn, and hay used as fodder for the farm animals, had to be stacked for long periods, protection from the weather was largely the province of the thatcher, so much so that in some cases he would specialize almost exclusively in this work. (On some farms, however, this task would be carried out by that most versatile and much undervalued worker, the farm-hand.) Stack-thatching brings into play a repertoire of tools and a technique all its own.*

A ladder rested against the side of a stack has not the same degree of security that is given by the side of a house; in order to keep it in place a stack-pin was driven between the rungs into the stack. The early form consisted of a stout iron spike affixed to a wooden shaft, in all about five feet in length, the head with a wooden peg to hold the ladder. The later version, the ladder-hook, was entirely of iron, with a strong recurved hook which not only secured the ladder, but allowed it to be turned over, so that the hook need only be withdrawn and re-positioned on alternate shifts. The yealms of straw were held on a large bracket, hooked into the stack, and known as a stack cradle. Two of these were collected for the Museum of East Anglian Life from a farm on the Suffolk–Norfolk border, at Ilketshall St Margaret, and others were filmed only a few years ago on a farm in Essex, where farming with horses is still carried out, and there is therefore the need for straw. Straw rope was also used to suspend weights to hold down the tarpaulins used as stack-covers.

* An excellent account of stack-thatching with long straw is given by Thomas Potts in *The British Farmers Cyclopaedia* (2nd Edition, 1808) – '. . . in order to confine the thatch in its place, straw ropes are laid along the top and eaves, being pinned with pointed sticks'. Straw ropes were made with the scud-winder.

Some idea of the great rise in the cost of thatching may be gained from the early account books which have fortunately survived. Charles Freeman, of Stowupland Hall, kept regular details of expenditure in his diaries.* His house was slated, so presumably a payment to a thatcher, Abbott of Earl Stonham, of £3 for sixty squares† at 1s. 8d. a square was either for a barn or for stacks. Frank Linnett, whose grandfather and father thatched in Essex, and later in Suffolk, has preserved the day books of his forbears. In 1948, his father thatched a stack for 6s. 6d. a square, and a cottage for 4s. 6d. The cost of the latter, after adding materials, came out to £50; an estimate given in 1974 for the same work was between £700 and £800. Haystacks had to be thatched, but for some reason were done for much less than straw, about 1s. 6d. compared with 6s. 6d.

Owing to the difficulty of obtaining suitable straw, noted above, it is unusual in these days to see a complete roof actually in process of thatching with straw. It was only after this account had been written that the writer was fortunate in coming across such a case. It was a small cottage, and although the thatch was badly in need of renovation, it had not proved necessary to remove the old material entirely. Once the worn layers had been pulled away, the process was as follows:

The new straw was pulled out in handfuls, and as each bundle was laid in place, beginning as always at the eaves, it was temporarily held in place by driving in *liggers*, or needles, whichever happened to be handy. The straw was then secured by driving in *broatches*, each made by a deft twist of a ligger of a length of two feet. A beechwood mallet was used to drive them into the thatch. The temporary stays were then removed.

The result was a type of long-straw thatch, but no attempt was made to give it the fine finish commonly seen in the older examples of this type; however, no doubt it served its purpose of keeping out the wet and cold, and indeed the excessive heat of the summer sun. It is this quality of maintaining a happy mean that is the attractive feature of thatch.

---

* The diaries of Charles Freeman, kept from 1820 to 1830, and his son William, 1851–1857, were presented to the Abbot's Hall Museum by Miss Joyce Freeman, grand-daughter of William.
† A square of thatch is one square yard.

VII
Rake & Scythe-stick Maker, Thatching Spar Maker, Hurdle Maker

Hark! where the sweeping scythe now rips along
Each sturdy Mower, emulous and strong,
Whose writhing form meridian heat defies,
Bends o'er his work, and every sinew tries.
ROBERT BLOOMFIELD (1766–1823)

The tools and methods used in these crafts have so much in common that they seem to fall naturally into a group of their own. They are well summed up in the words of Frank William Bird, rake- and scythe-stick-maker of Sicklesmere in West Suffolk:

'My father worked in the woods but he was not a rake-maker or a scythe-stick-maker; he was a *brawtch* and thatching-peg river; he was not a hurdle-maker, but my grandfather was a hurdle-maker; I've done all those jobs',

The making of rakes and scythe-sticks seems to be invariably linked; hurdle-making and thatching-spar-making may be carried on as separate crafts, or may be found allied with other woodland activities. Working in wood brings an intimate knowledge of the material in its various forms; the craftsman can, and will if the occasion arises, turn his hand to the fashioning of products other than those regularly included in his repertoire, even though this means using his accustomed tools for work for which they are not intended. Frank Bird's father used a small adze for riving his thatching spars; the usual tool for this is a small bill-hook known as a *riving-hook*.

A particular interest lies in the fact that in East Anglia – in fact,

15 *The Rake- and Scythe-stick-maker's Tools*
1. Stail-engine 2. Draw-knife 3. Stock-knife 4. Driving-stool, peg-stool 5. Shaving-horse 6. Draw-knife (Nos 1, 2 & 6: 1/6; remainder 1/12)

E.A.C.—F

in Suffolk – were to be found the last of the rake- and scythe-stick-makers working purely manually, or practically so, Thomas Cutting, of Haughley,* whose work was cut off by his death in the 1950s, and the Welnetham Woodwork Company, where Frank Bird was employed until recently, and where a moderate degree of mechanization has been introduced, and had been in operation for some of the time that Thomas Cutting was still using the traditional methods.

Indeed it seems doubtful whether the peculiar qualities demanded, particularly in the scythe, could be produced satisfactorily by a completely mechanized system, and that used at Welnetham, although accelerating the processes, still leaves a great deal to the skill of the craftsman. What has in effect been done is to provide a source of power which can be harnessed to operate what are essentially only slightly modified versions of the hand-tools. The adequacy of these tools seems to be underlined by the fact that the Welnetham Company has now a virtual monopoly of the craft, not only in this country, but throughout the world.

It will perhaps be most profitable to examine first the materials, tools and methods used by the village rake- and scythe-stick-maker, and to follow this with a description of the modifications introduced as a result of mechanization. The day book of Samuel Rye, who founded the Haughley workshop in 1853, details the implements produced. There was the small hand rake in which the *stail*, often in East Anglia called simply *stick*, is set into the head at one point, and the *crotch* rake in which the stail is split up and spread to enter the head at two points. A larger version of this was the *hobby* rake or *moggy* rake, the most usual implement for the harvesting of hay. The fabrication of the long, curved tines for this rake defeated any attempt to mechanize the process. The *Dunmow* rake, made in the Welnetham workshop, and to be described later, was intermediate between the Haughley *crotch* rake and the *hobby* rake.

A great variety of products besides rakes and scythe-sticks came both from the Haughley workshop and that at Welnetham. *Beetles* or *mauls* were made, and are still in demand in large quantities;

---

* An account of the workshop of Thomas Cutting of Haughley has been given by T. W. Bagshawe in *Gwerin*, Vol. 1, No. 2, 1956; his tools are now in the Museum of East Anglian Life at Stowmarket, and are illustrated in the present writer's book, *Life and Tradition in Suffolk and North-East Essex*, Dent, 1976

flails for threshing the corn in the days before the *drum* was introduced, handles for hoes, hammers and axes, handles for forks, shepherds' crooks, and indeed almost any implement needing a handle – all were made by the rake-maker. In addition to the regular scythe-sticks, he made handles for sickles and reaping-hooks, and *cradles* for attachment to the scythe when reaping corn. For the farmer, he supplied pommeltrees and whippletrees for the attachment of harness for the plough and the harrow, plough-sticks to clear away the mud which accumulated as the plough turned up the furrow, *scuppits* for grain and for digging out the mud when cleaning the pond, *strikes* to level off the grain in the measure. He also made handles for the oven peels and forks used by the baker, and for the cooper, wooden *tap-sticks* to be fitted into the casks.

There is no precise record of the sources used by the Haughley craftsmen for their materials, though some woods in the area show indications of having been used for coppicing. The varieties of wood used seem to have been somewhat different, at least in proportion, from those in use at Welnetham. 'Rake handles or "sticks" were turned from ash, birch, willow, alder and hazel. . . . Scythe-sticks were shaped from alder, birch and willow'.* Some rakes were fitted with iron teeth, often nails, and these were made and supplied by the blacksmith, who also made the iron hoops for the *beetle*; these were fitted by the rake-maker, using a technique closely comparable with that used in putting on the iron tyre on a wagon wheel, though on a miniature scale. This process will more adequately be described in giving an account of beetle-making at Welnetham, where it was possible to see a demonstration.

Rake stails were most frequently made from ash, which has a growth which is well adapted to this use. The required length was cut off and placed in the *shaving-horse*, a long stool with an inclined table, on which the stick was rested, held firmly by a pivoted clamp operated by a foot-bar. This left both hands free for the operation of barking, which was carried out with a *round-shave*, a draw-knife with rounded blade. The stail was next placed in a vice, and rounded with the *stail-engine*, a plane consisting of two stocks hollowed out at the centre, with a blade, so that the stail passed through the aperture thus formed. The stail-engine was rotated by means of two handles. After Thomas Cutting took over the Haughley

* *Op. cit.*

workshop, he devised a form of lathe, driven by a small paraffin engine, which rotated the stail whilst the stail-engine was merely pushed forward to effect rounding. This seems to have been in effect a simple form of the apparatus used at Welnetham – the very beginning of mechanization.

The handles were then smoothed with *shagreen*, a form of shark-skin, as sandpaper was at that time deemed too expensive. If a crotch rake was in the making, a cut of the required length provided for eventual spreading of the tips.

If the stick was in need of straightening, this was carried out on a bending horse, which made it sufficiently supple to be manipulated.

The head, of ash, was cut on the saw-bench, and holes were bored out with the spiral-auger to take the tines. These were also of ash; they were sawn and riven to approximate size, and driven through the *driving-stool* with a mallet. The driving-stool or *peg-stool* is in effect a tubular plane, a steel tube set vertically in the stool, with the upper edge sharpened. Next the pegs are driven into the head, and must then be sharpened. This is done on the *tooth-stool*, or *stock-knife* (much the same implement as that used by the clog-maker). Each tooth is held in turn in a grooved block at the front of the stool, and cut to a point with the long, pivoted knife. (A completely different method is used at Welnetham.)

Scythe-stick-making at Haughley had not attained any great degree of specialization; a scythe was – a scythe. Occasionally the craftsman undertook to supply the whole scythe, complete with blade and *tacks*, but more usually he confined himself to the making of the stick and tacks, the blade being fitted, and the scythe *hung* by the blacksmith. The reason for this was two-fold: the *irons* for the *tacks* were, of course, made by the blacksmith, and *hanging* the scythe was a complicated affair, as the tacks had to be adjusted to meet the requirements of the individual who was to use the scythe, be he tall or short. The tail of the stick was rested on the shoulder, and the position for the first tack was found by taking the position of the extended finger-tips; the second tack was placed at the distance measured from the finger-tips to the elbow.

The woods used for scythe-sticks at Haughley were alder, birch and willow, whereas ash was much more used for the purpose at Welnetham. In order to make them pliable for bending to shape, the sticks were placed in a *steam-box*, twelve feet in length by

one foot three inches wide, and one foot six inches deep. Water
was heated in a copper to produce steam, which was passed through
a hole into the box, which could accommodate four dozen rake-
sticks and thirty scythe-sticks at a time. After steaming the rake-
sticks were limbered up in the bending horse, the scythe-sticks
placed in the *press*, a horizontal stand with three rungs. The sticks
were passed under the uppermost rung, over the second, and lashed
to the third with rope. Bagshawe* gives the dimensions as seven
feet nine inches wide, and three feet high at the top end.

Whereas at Haughley the rake-maker purchased his wood from
local woodsmen, at Welnetham it was coppiced in the adjacent
Felsham Hall and Monkspark woods, and thereby hangs the tale
of a successful essay in preservation, both of the woods and the
craft.

In the later years of the nineteenth century John Last, a rake-
and scythe-stick-maker, was working at Lawshall in West Suffolk.
He was succeeded by his two nephews, A. and M. Last, who were
supplying their products to John George and Sons, a firm of iron-
mongers and hardware dealers, trading throughout eastern and
south-east England, from whom, in turn, the Last brothers purchased
such ironmongery as they required. The balance of this mutual
trading proved to be in favour of the larger firm, and debts piled
up for the Lasts. Finally, an agreement was reached by which
John George took over the Lasts' business, and in 1912 a workshop
was established at Little Welnetham, one of the brothers being
appointed as manager.

Mr George enjoyed the pursuits of the countryside, and had
bought from the local brewery company, Messrs Greene, King, Ltd.
of Bury St Edmunds, the neighbouring Monkspark and Felsham
Hall woods, thus satisfying his aspirations as a country landowner,
and at the same time providing a source from which, by coppicing,
he could obtain the material for the production of rakes and scythes.

By the 1930s, full-time woodsmen, to the number of a score or
more, were employed in coppicing, and the factory, if such it might
be called, was flourishing. A decade later, however, the increase
of mechanization in farming seemed to spell doom for the crafts,
but this was followed by an unexpected upsurge as horticulturists,
parks, and other purchasers found that the old and tried tools –

* *Op. cit.*

simple, durable, and comparatively cheap – had qualities far surpassing the products mass-produced by the large factories.

It would seem to be in some part the result of the fusion of two different disciplines which brought about, not so much a system of mechanization, but the adaptation of the traditional tools to methods of operation using other than simple hand-power, whilst at the same time leaving the quality of the product largely dependent on the skill of the craftsman. The tools were harnessed, by means of a system of lay shafts and belts, to a twelve-horse-power Hornsby paraffin engine, vaporization being assisted in the first place with the use of a blow-lamp, following which 'a swing on the wheel and she'd start off'.

Following a fire in 1939, this engine was replaced by a Blackstone diesel engine which proved more reliable, and further adaptations were possible.

Whatever the cause, however, and despite apparent regular demand for the workshop's products, by the 1960s the firm had gone into voluntary liquidation.

To make matters worse, it was intended to destroy Monkspark wood, and plough up the land, and it would appear that the County Council had given planning consent; Felsham Hall wood was in danger of a similar fate; thus a thriving craft, and its source of materials, seemed to be doomed. The woods, moreover, were the habitat of several rare plants. The situation was eventually saved, after a long tussle with unsympathetic authorities, through the efforts of local historians and naturalists, in co-operation with Dr and Mrs J. W. Litchfield, who had recently come to live in the district, and who offered to buy the factory subject to the woods being offered for sale to the Society for the Promotion of Nature Reserves, and for five years Mrs Litchfield ran the enterprise with ever increasing success. She had the benefit of the services of two experienced craftsmen, Frank William Bird, and Noël Cullum, the latter of whom continues to work under the present proprietor, Mr R. Hack. To all of them, this account of the history and work of the factory owes a great deal. The craft has not only been saved, but it now holds a unique position; the woods are gradually returning to full use as a source of materials for the rakes and scythe-sticks.

A great many varieties of wood can be used, especially for rake handles. Frank Bird listed ash, birch, alder, sycamore, elm (though not by preference), hazel, willow, some maple, and *gutridge* (dog-wood).* When seeking information on the properties of the various woods, the rake-maker will be able to give you the answer; no other craftsman has experience of so many species. Cutting must not be done whilst the sap is running, which would point to winter as the best season, but 'early cutting is better than late'; the flow slackens sooner than is often thought to be the case, in late August, and begins again earlier than is often realized. If whilst cutting a way through the undergrowth, a maple branch is lopped, as early as February, sap will drip freely.

In some ways a comparison may be made between coppicing and the cutting of the osiers, but with the latter the growth needed is thin, and the cutting takes place annually, an upward stroke ensuring an oblique surface to the stool, so that the rain will not rot the stump. Ash, and similar woods are best cut at a growth of ten or eleven years, and cutting is done with a bill-hook or axe. The original sapling, grown from the seed, is known as *ground ash* or *maiden ash*, successive growths from the stool as *stub ash*; in due course, one stool will if left undisturbed produce a ring, some three or four feet in diameter, of tall, straight growths suitable for rake handles. Ash is generally a white wood, but a variety is found which shows reddish in section; it is reputed to be stronger than the white, and the cut wood has a pleasant aroma. Unless it is urgently needed, ash is not stripped of its bark until after it has passed through the steam-box, and winter-cut ash is placed in the steam-box at least by March, as after cutting it is liable to attack by the *ash-fly*, one of the burrowing beetles of the family *Scolytidae*.

After steaming, the rake *stail* may need to be straightened; it is passed through the bending horse, an upright Y-shaped fork made from a stout natural forked branch, standing about four feet to four feet six inches high, with a cross-bar to give leverage so as to loosen the stick.

It is then secured in the *chuck* of the rounding machine, and passed through the cutter, which is in effect a *stail-engine* of much the same type as that used at Haughley, the difference being that here the stail is rotated, and the cutter simply pushed forward by the operator along its length. The cutter has two blades, the for-ward one being a *jacking* blade to cut away the surplus wood, the rear blade adapted for smoothing. Final smoothing is carried out, not

* A name also used for the spindle-tree.

as at Haughley with *shagreen*, nor with sandpaper, but with a sanding machine, run off a belt as in the case of all or most of the implements.

If the rake is to be of the *crotch* variety, made with a *straddle*, i.e. the stail divided and entering the head at two points, the necessary cut is made on the circular saw, and the degree of accuracy attainable with this tool is remarkable. The head, of ash, is cut, and bored on an ingenious machine invented, (curiously enough as he was essentially a *hand* craftsman), by the one of the Last brothers who took over management of the factory when it was founded. In the case of a straight stail, the holes for the teeth must be bored at a slight angle to give the necessary tilt.

Another remarkable device is that used, in place of the more primitive *froe*, to cut the pegs for the teeth. It is made from an old *portable* engine (which may once have driven a threshing drum), laid on its side, the piston cut and adapted as a ram to drive the blocks of ash, six inches long, of square section, on to a blade which rives them into pegs. These are then placed in another machine which performs a similar function to the *driving-stool* used at Haughley, rounding the teeth. Next, these must be driven into the head, which is secured by a clamp. The head is next laid on a shelf, roughly breast-high, and held firmly by an upright stake wedged under another shelf above; the teeth are then sharpened with a draw-knife, in place of the traditional stock-knife. Teeth for the large *hobby rake* are curved, and must be cut separately with the draw-knife.

For most of the rakes in general production the head was of a uniform length of twenty-eight and a half inches, and the teeth six inches. The manner of setting gave the variation needed for the function intended. The seed-rake had nineteen teeth, the stail cut to straddle five teeth. A rake for leaves with seventeen teeth and a hay-rake with fifteen teeth could also be used for general purposes. The Old English Rake had fourteen teeth, the outer set an inch and a half from the ends; the straddle was of only two teeth, and the rake was regarded as exceptionally strong. Two popular types are the *Dunmow*, with fourteen teeth set in at two and a half inches, and the *Rochford* with eleven teeth; hazel was found to be satisfactory for the stails of these, and later replaced ash. The tip of the Dunmow stail was pointed; it could be stuck upright into the ground when not in use. A garden rake was made with a twenty-inch head and thirteen teeth, and a *twitch* rake with twelve five-inch metal teeth, to deal with the troublesome couch grass. A rake with twelve galvanized teeth had a twenty-six-inch head, with the stail let into a single hole, and held by two diagonal wire strands.

Five different patterns of scythe-stick are made at Welnetham, though the main production seems now to be concentrated on the *American*; this five-foot stick is popular, as its sinuous form allows the user to remain in a more upright posture than do the traditional forms. Of this, Frank Bird had something to say:

'The old scythe users, they used to like the *fleeter** ones, particularly, because they was never afraid to get down, you see, that was the rhythm.' The American *snead* is five feet in length, and is invariably of ash (although apparently elm has been tried out). The softwoods are not suited to take the necessary degree of bending. Great care must be taken if it is necessary to thin down; wood is never taken from the outside of the bend; this would cause collapse by cutting across the fibres where they are tensed. The blade may be secured by a ring, as in other scythes, but the *loop* is more usual; the foot is flattened laterally, and a plate let in to one side, a loop passing through this to the other side to take the prong of the blade.

The English scythe has a length of six feet; the foot is thick and rounded, and the whole stick almost straight for its distal half; it has lost its appeal since the introduction of the American type. The old scythe-users were not only partial to the *fleeter* scythe, of which this is an example, but could bear the strain of the longer, four-foot blade, now replaced by one of three feet.

In Norfolk and Suffolk, until the advent of the American scythe, one known in Norfolk as the *Norfolk*, and in Suffolk as the *Suffolk* was favoured; it is still made. It has much the same profile as the English scythe, but is slightly shorter, five feet ten inches, and the last foot or so is hexagonal in section, and ends in a point.

The *Northampton* scythe resembles the Suffolk, but with a rather more wavy contour, though less so than the American.

Last of the five now in production, though by no means least, is the *roding* scythe. The name is not one which is to be found in any of the dictionaries of dialect, at least not in this connection, but

* Principal authorities on dialect give *fleeter* = shallower. Here obviously it can be rendered as straighter.

some enlightenment is given in an entry in the accounts of the Commissioners of the Lakenheath and Brandon District: *

1782. Jan. 21. to Rodeing the Turfon Drain.

The scythe is used for trimming the growth on the banks of drains, from the top of the bank. It is lowered so that the blade lies horizontally and is drawn upwards for cutting; it therefore needs to be of considerable length, and a ten-foot stick or even one of fourteen feet was not unknown. This proved a problem at Welnetham, where the steam-box would not take more than an eight-foot stick, but this was overcome by inserting the sticks as far as they would, and wrapping the projecting ends in sacking, closing the door of the box as far as possible. With such a length, it is practically useless to provide *tacks* or *nibs*, as the handles are called, though sometimes one was fitted. It was by no means unusual for the watermen to cut their own sneads from a nearby wood.

Although ash was the most favoured wood, and used practically without exception for the American scythe, the lighter woods such

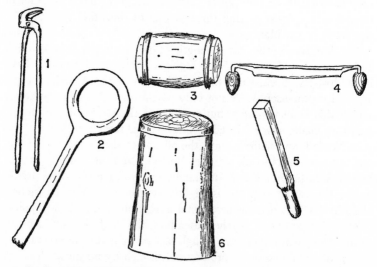

16   *Tools used in making beetles*
    1. Tongs   2. Handled ring   3. Head of beetle, with rings in place
    4. Draw-knife   5. Striker, for use with handled ring   6. Block   (All 1/12)

* West Suffolk Record Office EL97/13/43.

as birch or alder, especially the latter, were often used for the longer scythes such as the Norfolk or Suffolk, birch for the roding scythe.

The scythe-stick-maker, of course, also makes the *tacks*, and for this purpose a most ingenious cutter has been evolved, with blades set on a revolving drum at different angles. The fitting of the tacks, a process known as *hanging* the scythe, was performed by the blacksmith.

The *stocks* in which the sneads were bent to shape after steaming had, of course, to be differently constructed for the different types.

It will have been observed that some of the tasks carried out by the rake- and scythe-stick-maker, e.g. the making of beetles and some other tools, were also regularly performed by the wheelwright. It is perhaps significant that the bill-hook used by the rake-maker, like the axe of the wheelwright, is bevelled only on the right of the blade (or on the left for a left-handed man). Faggot-making is one of his side-lines, and the small hook on the back of the blade is designed for this purpose.

The beetle is a heavy wooden maul, or mallet, designed for use where a sledge-hammer cannot be used, but considerable force is needed; it was employed, with a wooden, iron-tipped wedge, for riving timber, and also in earlier times for cutting clay when *claying* of the land was regularly carried out as a means of improving its fertility.

The head consists of a block of wood, often elm; two sizes are usually made, one of diameter of six inches, and a foot long, and another of ten inches with a five and a half inch diameter. At Welnetham, where more sophisticated apparatus is available than was the case in the older workshops, the head of the beetle begins as a piece of squared timber of the length required. The angles are planed off, giving it an octagonal section, and this is reduced to a cylinder, reduced at the ends to give a slightly barrel form, to ensure a close fitting of the two iron hoops which prevent splitting when the beetle is in use. The rings are made by the blacksmith, but are fitted by the rake-maker. They are heated in the furnace which heats the boiler of the steam-box, extra heat being obtained by adding coke to the fire, for which wood is the usual fuel. As many as ten rings can be heated at one time. The head is now placed on end on a low wooden block. A ring is taken from the furnace and placed over the end; it is beaten on using a handled iron ring and a heavy bar, of square section, rounded at one end to form a handle. The head is then quickly plunged into water, to cool and shrink the ring, in the same way as the tyre fitted to a wagon wheel.

THE HURDLE-MAKER

Until comparatively recently some wattle hurdles were made by the basket-maker, whose principal material, the osier, lent itself well to the manufacture of small hurdles such as those used by the horticulturist for plant protection. The hurdle-maker proper was

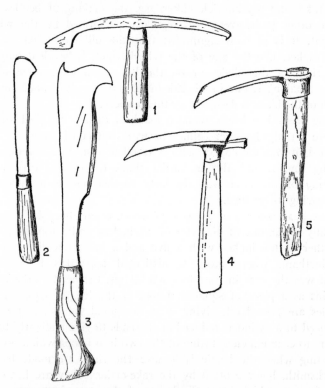

17 *Tools used in making Thatching-spars and Hurdles*
   1. Hurdle-maker's *tomahawk* – for morticing   2. Riving-hook used by a
   thatcher for making spars and broatches   3. Bill-hook   4. Small adze
   used by a woodman for making thatching-spars   5. Small adze used
   by a hurdle-maker for making broatches   (All 1/6)

concerned rather with the larger hurdles required by the farmer and stockbreeder.

These are of two kinds, wattle-hurdles and gate-hurdles, and whereas in some other parts of the country their making is regarded as the province of two different craftsmen, in East Anglia this is not the case, both being made by one man. Materials, too, differ in this region from those used elsewhere. For example, the principal wood used in the south of England for the fashioning of gate-hurdles was willow; in East Anglia it is ash, although other woods may be used when ash is difficult to obtain. This may be due to the fact that ash was commonly coppiced in East Anglia for the making of rakes and scythe-sticks. It is logical, therefore, to find it being used for the uprights at least of the wattle-hurdles as well as for gate-hurdles.

At the present time there would appear to be only two hurdle-makers working in East Anglia; at Barrow, in West Suffolk, there is a small factory specializing in the craft, but the last of the traditional village hurdle-makers would seem to be the brothers Lambert at Topcroft in Norfolk. They do not confine themselves to this work, but will make a rustic-seat, or a bird-table, or a besom for sweeping the lawn. In fact their guiding principle seems to be to use any wood which will serve for the purpose, and make anything for which the available wood proves suitable.

The material for wattle-hurdles consists normally of ash for the uprights, and hazel for the weave, but any straight shaft can be made to serve for the upright, and some of the hurdles examined were woven entirely of elm. Similarly with the gate-hurdles – any wood which would rive satisfactorily could be used; ash, or elm, or even maple. For the weave, suppleness is the main requirement.

The most notable tool seemed to be an axe of such proportions as to make one wonder whether the slight figure of the craftsman could wield it. Mortices were cut with a chisel, not with the *tomahawk*, formerly a characteristic implement of the hurdle-maker.

Wattle-hurdles could be made of any size required by the customer; some of those seen were up to eight feet in height and ten or twelve long.

There is a standard size for the gate-hurdle – a length of six feet, and a height of four feet, or sometimes four feet six inches. Three uprights are made, of split ash stakes. Into the cut side of each are cut mortices to take six bars, the lower more closely spaced than the upper. Diagonal braces run from the bottom of the outer uprights to the top of the centre.

Birch was at one time the universal material for the besom; scarcity has necessitated the substitution of hazel in recent times.

THE THATCHING-SPAR-MAKER

Strictly speaking, there is no such craft in East Anglia, but if for some reason the thatcher did not choose to rive his own *sways* and *liggers*, he would seek the services of some other worker in wood. It might be the wheelwright, or the basket-maker, but as often as not it would be the rake-maker. The material used was hazel; the *sways* varied in length according to need; the *liggers* were usually two feet in length, and could conveniently be twisted to form *broatches*.

Various tools were used, according to the craftsman's usual practice. In some cases, a small *bill-hook* or *riving-hook* was favoured, but one woodman, who was a hurdle-maker, reserved a small adze for the purpose, and this was passed on to his son, who was himself a rake-maker. This, and the riving-hook, possessed the advantage over the *froe* of the wheelwright, that it could also be used to point the ends of the spar.

VIII
The Osier-Basket Maker & the Rush Weaver

The East Anglian will stoutly deny the common assumption that his region is flat; indeed, although it has not the steep gradients of the moors, or Lakeland, it is on the whole gently rolling and by no means monotonous. Nevertheless it is much intersected by rivers, whose flood-plains provide ideal ground for reeds and willows, whilst the streams themselves form a natural habitat for many species of rush. It is in such conditions that the craft of the osier-basket-maker is able to flourish and the rush-weaver garner the materials he needs. From every point of view, and not least the aesthetic, it is to be regretted that these craftsmen have to face the fierce competition of the manufacturer of the unpleasing and apparently indestructible plastic container.

THE OSIER-BASKET-MAKER

The site chosen for the osier bed must be of sufficient size to allow for a period of fallowing. The ground is deep-ploughed, and thoroughly manured; meantime the *sets* are prepared by cutting up willow rods, of a selected stock, into lengths of approximately one foot, each bearing a number of buds. These are planted by pushing into the ground for about half their length, at intervals of a foot, with two feet or so between rows to allow for hoeing, which is now carried out for the most part by machine. It is important to keep the ground free of weeds if a good healthy growth is to be obtained.

Winter is the best time for planting, so that the spring flow of the sap will cause the buds to develop, those below ground forming roots, those above, shoots.

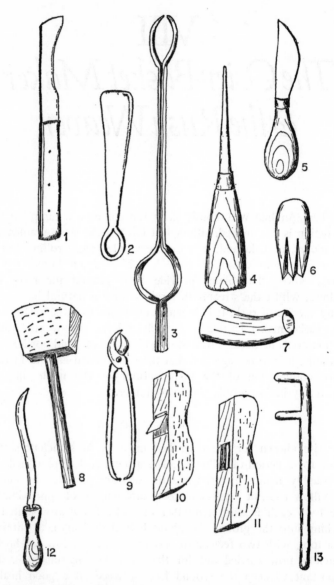

18 *The Osier-basket-maker's Tools*
  1. Picking-knife 2. Shop-iron 3. Brake, willow-stripper 4. Bodkin
  5. Pinking-knife 6. Cleaver 7. Grease-horn 8. Mallet 9. Shears
  10. Shave 11. Cane-rive 12. Shell-bodkin, cane-pinker 13. Commander
  (Nos 1, 4, 5, 6, 7, 10 & 11 : 1/3; 2, 3, 8, 9, 12 & 13 : 1/6)

After the initial preparation of the land, further manuring is not generally necessary; the falling leaves produce all the compost needed to maintain healthy development.

Although the natural habitat is on low, moist ground, and this is where the more long-established osier beds are to be found, one grower reports great success on higher land, provided it is in good heart. A disadvantage here, however, is that irrigation may be necessary in an exceptionally dry period.

The crop will not be in full production for some three years, but must still be cut each autumn to encourage fresh growth. As in all shrubs, pruning stimulates growth.

Harvesting takes place in the late autumn and winter, preferably after a frost, which will encourage leaf-fall. This is desirable

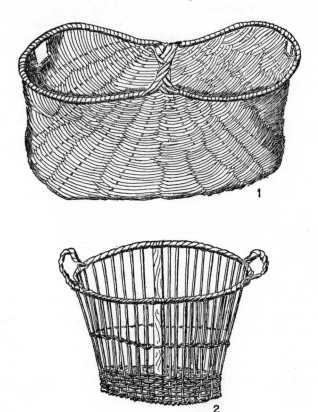

19 'Swill' (1) and Quarter-cran Basket (2) (Scale: 1/12)

not only to obtain the benefit of the leaves as compost, but it is easier to cut and handle the rods when they are clear of leaf. The rods are cut individually, using a hook with a short, broad blade (often ground down to shorten it for convenience of working in the comparatively cramped space). It is a process requiring considerable skill and practice. A short, sharp upward stroke is used, as close to the stool as possible. This leaves a clean, oblique surface, from which the rain will drain, thus avoiding any danger of the stool becoming waterlogged, and rot setting in. Cutting must be complete, so that the new growth will develop strong and straight for the next season.

Cropping may go on for a number of years, but eventually the bed will show signs of exhaustion. It is then cleared, and some other crop, often potatoes, will be grown for the next three years to clear the land ready for re-planting. On an old-established osier bed in Suffolk, held in the same family for several generations, the practice was to maintain ninety-five acres of the hundred acre plot in full production, while the other five acres had their period of rest. The bed had thus a continuous working life of about sixty years.

Several different species of the genus *Salix* have been found suitable for growing to produce rods; the most usual appears to be the Common Sallow (*Salix atrocinerea*, Brot.), though the Great Sallow (*Salix capraea*, L.), popularly known as the Pussy Willow from its furry catkins, is also used in East Anglia, and a variety known as Black Maul is popular with the basket-maker; it has a relatively small pith which makes it strong and resilient.

Three grades of material are produced, in no way corresponding to the different species used, but dependent on the treatment to which they are subjected:

Brown Willow
This is dried without removal of the peel or bark; the rods are cut and stood out to dry naturally, the colour gradually changing from the natural green, through yellow, to brown. Its natural use is for such items as baskets for outdoor use, and for wickerwork furniture, but public demand encourages the basket-maker to interweave it with other grades to form an attractive pattern.

Buff Willow
The willow is boiled for several hours in a long tank, and left to

soak, when the wood absorbs some of the tannin of the bark, giving it the *buff* colour. It is then ready for stripping. The traditional method is by the use of the *willow-stripper* or *brake*, a stout steel rod with forked tip, or a pair of rods mounted together to give the same effect. The *brake* is fixed in an upright stock. The heel of the rod is pressed against the fork to start the peel, and the rod then reversed and drawn through the fork to strip the peel. Sometimes several brakes will be mounted side by side in a long *horse*, so that a number of workers, usually women, can operate together. A more usual piece of apparatus in modern times is a rotary drum, driven by a small diesel or petrol engine; the drum bears rows of forks, and the rods are pushed into it, passing through to the other side, the stripping complete. It was interesting to find that an old-established willow grower, whose family had been in the craft for several generations, had tried out such a drum in the 1930s, but had found the older method preferable, even though slower, whilst another maker, coming into the field in recent years, had automatically taken up the newer mode and found it completely satisfactory.

White Willow

White Willow is probably the most used of the three grades; the manner of its production is much the most elaborate. After cutting, the rods are soaked and stood in shallow troughs, in the open. Spring brings a renewed flow of sap; rootlets are formed, and fresh foliage develops. By late May or early June they are ready for the stripper, which leaves them pure and white, and ready for use.

Although from the nature of his craft, the osier-basket-maker was usually to be found in rural districts, his wares were not produced only for local consumption. True, in the days when agricultural methods were themselves 'traditional', the local countryside provided its quota of customers. The large winnowing-basket, or chaff-basket, was made here, as were baskets for fruit-picking and the potato-harvest, baskets for the butcher, and the grocer's errand-boy, but others went far afield. At one time, one maker in Suffolk supplied practically all the baskets for Smithfield Market, and for the fish-merchants. Large, square baskets were made for the laundries, and for the travelling salesman, whose wares would be wheeled through the streets as he trudged beside it on his way to call on his customers. The *cran* in which the catches of herring were landed were largely the work of a specialist in this particular field.

As the production of the willow rods depended so much on the skill of the grower, so did the making of his wares. The tools of the craft are few and simple. When working, the basket-maker sits on the floor with a large board, the *lap-board*, resting on his knees, a method of working which may seem awkward and uncomfortable to the onlooker, but which has remained constant throughout the generations, and must therefore be presumed to have been found the most effective.

The shears used for cutting the rods to the required length have short broad blades, rather resembling a pair of garden secateurs, but much longer in the handles. When finer material is called for, the rods are split with the *cleaver*, a small wooden egg-shaped implement, the rounded butt fitting the palm of the hand, the distal end narrowing and cut into four, or sometimes three teeth. Pressure with this on the end of the rod divides it evenly into sections, known as *skeins*. Before use, the sharp edge of the skein must be removed, and this is done with the *shave*, a midget plane, four inches in length, the stock rounded and shaped to fit the palm. Further trimming, to ensure an even thickness throughout the length of the skein, is carried out with another tool, the *cane-river*, similar in appearance to the *shave*, but with two parallel blades between which the skein passes as it is trimmed.

A tool which is somewhat curiously named as a *shell-bodkin* is in effect a knife, with a fine, sinuous blade some seven inches or so in length; its alternative name, the *cane-pinker*, more accurately conveys its function. A short, stout *pinking-knife*, with a blade two and a half inches long and one and a half inches wide, is needed for trimming in the final stages of making the basket.

As fresh rods are added to the weave, the tension naturally increases, and with it the difficulty of the work; the *bodkin* used to open up the space between the rods to allow of the insertion of fresh material is a sturdy implement, with a blade of six inches or more, made from half-inch iron bar, rounded towards the point. The ash handle, secured by a strong iron ferrule, showed signs in one example examined of having been beaten through on occasion, the wood having been frayed by repeated blows. The blade is periodically lubricated by dipping in the grease-horn or grease-hole.

As weaving proceeds, the rods must be beaten in so as to mould the basket to shape; this is done with the *shop-iron*, a triangular iron bar ten or twelve inches long, increasing from a spherical butt to a distal width of some two inches.

From time to time, the vertical rods of the basket must be straightened, and for this the *commander*, a thick rod of iron terminating in a U-shaped bend, comes into service; it is also used as a beater on occasion.

With few exceptions, baskets are made from the base upwards, the technique depending on the shape.

Several rods, the number varying according to the intended size of the basket, are placed crosswise over one another to form the *slath*; this should be formed of stout rods; a thinner rod, the weaver, is then passed behind one leg of the slath, and the ends twisted as they pass between the rods. In this manner a base is formed, with the ends of the rods of the slath projecting. These are turned up to form the *upset*, a term which is self-explanatory, and the making of the sides proceeds by intertwining fresh weavers. At this stage upright *stakes* are inserted at intervals, and the weaving proceeds round these.

Different patterns of weave are used. In forming the *upset*, it is usually desirable to have a close mesh, and two or more rods may be passed through alternately between the stakes. In *fitching* and *pairing*, the weavers are worked alternately over and under each other so that at each stroke a stake is gripped. Such a technique is suitable for a basket such as the *quarter-cran*, where the sides are to be comparatively open. In *randing* a single weaver passes alternately in front and behind each stake, and in *slewing* the same technique is used with two weavers. A stout base can be obtained by using the process of *waling*, in which several weavers, often three or even more, pass outside two or three stakes and behind the next.

There are some exceptions to the technique described above. When the basket is to be of square shape, the corner rods are held in a clamp, and the rods woven round them. The fisherman's *swill*, to be mentioned later, is made by forming the rim first; from this stakes are bowed round to give the bag-like shape, and the weavers worked across these.

Regrettably, more and more baskets are being superseded by factory-made containers of synthetic materials, and the craft is being kept alive largely by those interested in carrying it on for aesthetic rather than practical reasons. It would be a pity if the hand-made basket should ever lose its appeal. It has given occupation, and income, to many who, through loss of sight, or due to other handicap, are unable to carry on more arduous work.

The specialization of the individual basket-maker is governed by the nature and needs of the area where he lives and works. In an agricultural district the demands on his services were greater in the past than now; the great winnowing baskets are things of the past; so are the clothes-baskets for the housewife; now they are ugly contrivances of some sort of plastic, light and handy, no doubt, but not evocative of any feeling of satisfaction in good craftsmanship. On the coast, in the abundant days of the herring fishery, the call was for two baskets of individual and pleasing design. First came the *swill*, of valise-like form, so that a pair could conveniently be loaded, pannier fashion, on a donkey or pony, to transport the herring direct from the beach where the longshore fishermen landed their catch. The swill has been attributed by some writers exclusively to Suffolk; it was in fact used as far north as Wells on the North Norfolk coast, and at Great Yarmouth, as the regular container in use for the herring as they were unloaded at the quayside; the fish were sold directly from the swill. It was followed by the *quarter-cran* basket (the *cran*, consisting approximately of one thousand herring, varying according to the size of the fish, was the unit of measurement adopted for the sale of the herring). The basket did not need to be closely woven for fish of this size, and the openwork sides made for lightness. It is possible to approximate the use of the swill with the era of the sail-driven fishing boat, the quarter-cran with the introduction of steam.

In the Fenland areas of Cambridgeshire, the long, flask-like *eel-hives* are made of basketry. The hive may be as much as five feet in length, though three feet is perhaps a more usual size. It consists of two chambers or *chairs*. The hive is closed at the top, from which extends a slender neck, expanding to form the *top chair*, with a diameter of about six inches (in the three-foot hive) at the halfway mark; it then contracts to a waist of approximately three inches, and expands to form the *bottom chair*, which narrows slightly to the base, which is of course open. The bait is placed in the *top chair*, and once the eel has been tempted into this portion, it cannot return, the waist forming a valve.

THE RUSH-WEAVER

The rush used for weaving is the true bulrush (*Scirpus lacustris*, L.), not to be confused with the reed-mace (*Typha latifolia*, L.), which is so commonly given the name. The two are only distantly related, belonging to different botanical families. The latter is easily distinguished by its large spectacular inflorescence; it is decorative rather than useful.

The rush grows in rivers and streams, and was formerly plentiful; its presence in the River Deben, in Suffolk, was responsible for the establishment of the Deben Rush-Weavers at Debenham, but the river now supplies no material to the weavers, and most supplies for the Suffolk craftsmen come from Northamptonshire and Bedfordshire. The weavers arrange all the cutting themselves, as they do for supplies from the Continent. This is the occasion for the organization of summer camps, and students form the bulk of the labour force. Nature takes no account of recent legislation on sex discrimination; boys are found to be naturally better at cutting, girls for tying the bundles. In theory, these should measure thirty-six inches in circumference (one authority goes so far as to stipulate thirty-seven inches!), but in practice bundling is, of course, arbitrary, though care will be taken to see that there are no serious discrepancies; payment is by the number of bundles made up in the day.

The reed grows under water; machine cutting has therefore been found to be impracticable. At St Ives, in Cambridgeshire, cutting is carried out from a boat, but this method is slow and therefore costly; it generally results in a yield of only eleven or twelve bundles as a result of a day's work.

A cutter wading into the water, knee-deep or often waist-deep, will cut up to one hundred bundles in a day. An ordinary reaping hook is used, and the cut is made as low as possible. The cut rushes are laid on the water, where they float; they are then gathered up into bundles, assembled in a 'raft', and floated down to a convenient place for removal. They are left on the bank for a few days to drain before transport to the factory, where they can be stood up to complete draining.

Cutting traditionally takes place 'between hay harvest and corn harvest'.

Heat is never used to accelerate drying; it would render the rush brittle. Even after drying, the production of a good rush depends much on the judgment and experience of the rush weaver. As in all crafts, success lies in the craftsman.

The material produced from all this careful preparation is not of uniform quality; the reed varies in thickness and in strength. The stiffer material is suitable for the loom, for weaving into mats; rather more pliable rushes can be used for seating chairs, and softer stems for plaiting and hand-weaving into various receptacles, baskets, hats, table mats, and so forth.

In readiness for making up the rush is dampened; some makers consider a quick immersion for ten or twelve minutes sufficient, but the Deben weavers have found that an overnight soaking gives better results.

Women are almost invariably employed in rush-weaving; they have on the whole a better touch for this work than men. It is found more practicable to employ workers of one sex, a mixture of the sexes for such work leads to so many administrative complications to comply with the numerous regulations which are imposed on industry, that in a comparatively small establishment it would add materially to the cost of production.

Almost the converse applies to the osier-basket-makers; men are far better equipped to cope with the problems of working with willow.

In one establishment, full-time employment throughout the year is found for a number of women, with one man who carries out the rougher work of cutting and drying. During the harvesting season, work is found usually for students who only want a part-time job during the vacation.

The 'Do-it-yourself' craze which has lately emerged, largely no doubt as a result of the inflated cost of getting the expert to do it, has had a curious effect; so many people have wanted to buy rushes to try their hand at reseating chairs, and other tasks, and have found that the results were not what they had hoped. They have then brought in their chairs for repair, and it has been found that they did not, in fact, realize the difference between cane and rush. So the rush-weavers turned their hands to cane-work. Then it was found that the chairs needed attention to the frame, and the result was the setting up of a complete service of repair and restoration under the same roof, thus in effect bringing about a craft centre where a number of crafts can be practised in association. This state of affairs is greatly to be preferred to the fate which has overtaken so many of our craftsmen, who have degenerated into salesmen for imported wares, often produced by processes far removed from the true crafts.

IX
Brick, Flint & Stone

There is no straw given unto thy servants, and they say to us, Make brick.

Exodus, Chapter V, verse 16

Before giving some account of brick-making in East Anglia, it is worth calling attention to a method of building which was more akin to that used in the time of the captivity of Israel in Egypt – clay lump. The clay, so plentiful in the region, was mixed with straw and often horse- or cow-dung, moulded into blocks varying in size from eighteen inches by twelve by six in Suffolk to twelve inches by six by six in Essex. These were sun-baked, and used frequently in building the walls of cottages, and even outside walls. The material was surprisingly durable, if treated with a coat of lime wash to keep out the wet, but a crack would let in the rain, and the whole structure was then liable to disintegrate. The manufacture of these blocks required no great skill, and could hardly be classified as a craft in its own right, but nevertheless was an integral feature of life in the region, and many buildings constructed in this way still remain.

Clay in various forms is plentiful throughout the region, and although brick-making lapsed for a spell after the departure of the Romans, it was revived at a very early date; at Coggeshall in Essex, bricks were made on the spot for the Abbey guest-house, built in 1190.

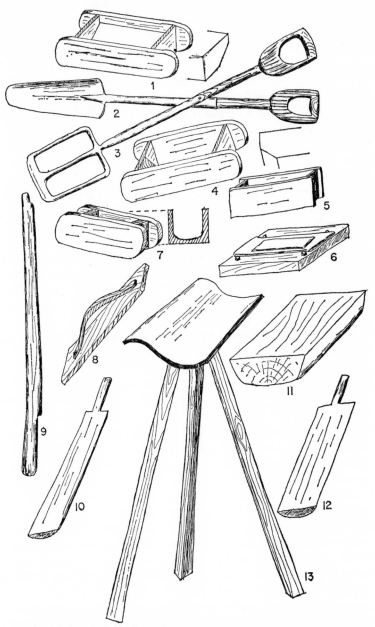

20 *The Brick-maker's Tools*
1. Mould for plinth   2, 3. Clay spades   4. Mould for return   5. Plain
brick mould   6. Stock for use with (5)   7. Mould for coping   8, 9. Strikes
10, 12. Bats   11. Stock for pantile   13. Trimming-plate for pantile   (Nos
1, 4, 5, 6, 7 : 1/9; remainder : 1/12)

The types of clay varied even within a relatively small area; for example, at Cove Bottom in Suffolk, and at nearby Frostenden, the clay was derived from silt laid down as a river bed. It was comparatively free from foreign matter, and needed very little treatment in the pug-mill to make it ready. A few miles away, on the other side of the marshes, lay Clay Common, where the blue clay had to be given considerably more thorough preparation to free it from the flints and pebbles, relics of its deposition in Glacial times. As it passed into the horse-driven pug-mill, water was pumped over it, and it emerged in liquid form, from which the water had to be drained.

Cove Bottom and Frostenden produced bricks of a rich red colour; those from Clay Common were white.

Traces of the horse-driven pug-mills used at Cove Bottom both for bricks and tiles may still be seen, a circle of bricks bedded into the ground marking the track. Since 1953, a modern pug-mill has been installed; it is driven by a diesel engine of eighteen horsepower.

From the mill, the blocks of clay passed to the brick-makers, who put it into moulds shaped according to the form intended – copings, both rounded and angled, jambs, plinths, and, of course, the plain wall bricks. The method used in making these will serve to illustrate the process in general. The apparatus is simple in form. A stock of wood, measuring ten and a half inches by six inches by two inches thick carries bolted to it an iron mould with a raised centre area which will form the frog of the brick; over this is placed a wooden box, iron-lined, the sides one foot by four inches high, with transverse iron walls set in to give a brick size of nine and a half inches by four and a quarter inches; shrinkage during drying will reduce the size by approximately a quarter of an inch all round. Into this mould the clay is pressed, any surplus being removed by means of a *strike*. Various forms of strike are found, but it was a not uncommon practice simply to pick up a *pallet* lying conveniently to hand, and level off with this. A stock of pallets would indeed be readily available, for this simple implement was necessary for the next stage; it was merely a flat board, one foot long and five inches wide and a quarter of an inch thick. This was placed on top of the brick in its mould which was then reversed, allowing the brick to rest on the pallet so that it could be removed without damage ready for removal to the drying sheds.

The 'green' bricks were piled on a hand-barrow and wheeled off to the sheds.

These are simply open-sided shelters, the roof supported at intervals by sturdy posts. They extend for a length of one hundred and eighty-five feet, and are fifteen feet six inches wide. The roof is low, to leave the bricks as little exposed to the weather as possible, five feet high to the eaves, ten feet to the ridge. Pantiles made on the site are used.

At Cove Bottom two of these sheds stand side by side and are interspersed with open drying areas of similar length; these had originally been on open ground, but it had been found of benefit in due course to concrete the areas to prevent rising damp. Under the sheds the bricks are piled to a height of eight bricks; in the open areas six bricks is the limit, and the green bricks are covered, both at Cove Bottom and at Tuddenham in Suffolk, with wooden tilts as a protection against rain. The procedure is to lay the whole of the bottom layer first so that by the time later layers are added some drying has taken place, reducing the danger of collapse. A sprinkling of sand lessens the risk of the bricks sticking together, or to the pallets.

The impression given to the onlooker is of a process simple in operation, but leisurely by comparison with mechanization; in fact, the speed with which bricks can be made by the expert is surprising; three men working steadily would regularly turn out two thousand bricks a day at the Cove Bottom brickworks; true, there were no restrictive practices, no remote chance of strikes, wildcat or otherwise.

The weather, to some extent, governed the progress of work, which was seasonal; the actual making began in March, and was discontinued during the winter months.

The need for speedy working will be appreciated when it is realized that the kiln accommodated some 33,000 bricks at one firing; stacking took three to four days, and firing occupied approximately one week.

The simple appearance of the kiln, viewed from the outside, when it looks for all the world like a small barn or stable, belies the spectacular interior. When the doors are opened it is seen that it extends as far below ground as above, the height being forty courses of bricks. The building occupies an area of twenty-seven feet by twenty-four feet at ground level. Each course of bricks is slightly inset so as to reduce the aperture at the top to some extent, and at one end is a series of steps to allow access to the top, where, in the final stages of stacking the kiln, a gable of loose bricks is erected to a height of four feet; a beam connects the two ends, and from this to the eaves, sloping planks are laid to close the aperture and form a roof.

Beside the kiln is a huge coal chute, fifteen feet six inches across, extending forward for eight feet, and about seven feet deep, with a narrow opening giving access to the stoke-hole. This lies behind the kiln, and is approached by a ramp. The eaves of the sloping, pantiled roof stand at seven feet; the wooden double doors, six feet in height, open to nine feet.

When the doors are opened, the stoke-hole is seen to extend for twenty-four feet, with a width of twelve feet; the roof is vaulted like a crypt, and rises to a height of some forty courses. In the rear wall are set the two furnaces, also arched to a height of some twenty-four courses, with rectangular openings at nine courses above the floor, and ash-pits below. Iron plates close the furnaces; these are suspended by chains, and swung aside during stoking, to be held by short chains secured by hooks in the wall. The extent of the furnaces may be gauged by the two iron rakes, one measuring twenty-two feet, and the other fifteen feet.

The bricks are piled in such a way as to leave an arch over the position of the fire-bars of the furnace, and are then stacked leaving an inch gap between bricks, the layers alternating in direction to give maximum draught. A small fire is lighted each day, and blocked up at night. This starts the drying process, and the furnace is operated at full draught once the stacking is completed. After a week's firing, the bricks closing the top are removed to allow cooling. Some of the bricks near the fire-bars may be scorched to a deeper tone; these are not regarded as spoilt, but are used in pattern-making during building.

In comparatively recent times, these bricks were occasionally fired in clamps; this method was used generally when only small quantities were wanted at short notice, and it was not worth while to fire the kiln.

At Cove Bottom, at least, the manufacture of pantiles was carried out in a self-contained unit, even to the extent of a separate pug-mill. The clay was rolled out in sheets, cut to the requisite size, moulded on a wooden template, and then reversed on a pallet in form rather like a short, broad cricket-bat. The tiles were then piled for drying in much the same manner as the bricks. A later development, to provide a more accurately finished article, was the use of an iron plate, shaped like a pantile, and mounted on a tripod. The tile was placed on this and the edges neatly trimmed with a knife.

The Cove Bottom brickworks are typical of the area in general. It was usual for each large estate to have its own brickworks, and even farmers occasionally had their own outfit, where the men might be occupied when other work was slack.* Frequently, too, as at Cove Bottom, the brickyard would be let on a tenancy. In the eighteenth and early nineteenth centuries the rent for a kiln, with house and two and a half acres of land, at Ardleigh in Essex, was 1s. 11d. per week; another, at Asheldam, was let for 2s. 4d., and yet another for 3s. 3d.*

Even in the present century wages were meagre; at Somerleyton in Suffolk, the 'wheeler' who transported the green bricks on a hand-barrow to the kiln was paid 2s. 6d. per thousand. A load consisted of sixty bricks each weighing nine pounds, and the narrow plank leading up to the kiln had to be taken at a run.†

Partly because, no doubt, the brickyard was originally designed to serve the needs of an estate rather than to enter a larger market, an optimum size seems to have evolved which could be run by two or three men, with some additional help at times, for it is interesting to find that works as far apart in our region as Cove Bottom and Fingringhoe in Essex had kilns with a capacity of 30,000 bricks. True, as demand increased some brickyards expanded to become industries serving a wide area. Woolpit in Suffolk became famous for its Suffolk Whites, though the once widely held belief that these were used for the building of the White House, home of the Presidents of the United States, appears to have been nothing more than a romantic wish.

The difficulty of obtaining stone for building was responsible for the earliest establishment of a brickyard in the region, if not in the country; the guest-house at Coggeshall Abbey was built in 1190, and all the evidence points to the bricks having been made

* A. F. J. Brown, *Essex at Work 1700–1815*, Essex Record Office Publications, No. 49, 1969.
† From an account of the Somerleyton Brickworks by Audrey and Arnold Butler, quoted in the *East Anglian Daily Times*, 22.7.76.

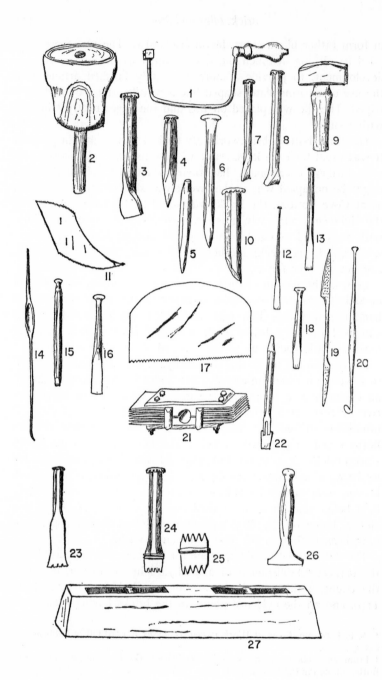

on the site. The same would appear to apply to Little Wenham Hall in Suffolk, built about a century later.

THE FLINT-KNAPPER

The dearth of quarryable building stone in the region was largely responsible for the persistence of timber-framed building construction, but from a very early period extensive use was made of one of the few materials yielded by the earth, the flint which was formed in the chalk, and mined by our Neolithic ancestors, who used it for weapons and tools. It is also found in quantity in the glacial clay derived from the chalk deposits.

It was used for building even in its rough state, as cobbles, but when dressed it provided an attractive and durable material for many of the buildings of East Anglia, more especially in Norfolk and Suffolk. In the churches in particular, combined with freestone, it gave scope for much imaginative design in flushwork.

The methods of dressing the flint differed from those used in Neolithic times only in the tools employed. Flint-knapping is still carried on at Brandon in Suffolk, though there is now little call for building blocks. Gun-flints are made, though no longer for arms in regular use; many go overseas for incorporation in replicas of ancient weapons made for the tourist trade.

In its hey-day, the craft provided not only dressed flints for building, and gun-flints, but strike-a-lights for the tinder-box.

THE STONEMASON

The geological history of East Anglia does not cover any period in which quarryable stone, either igneous or sedimentary, was laid down. True, some local deposits have yielded material suitable of use for building; the large concretions known as septaria, found in the deposits of London Clay, lend themselves to dressing for use as building stone, and have been used since Roman times.

21 *The Stonemason's Tools*
　　1. Brace 2. Mallet 3, 7, 8. Pitching tools 4, 5, 10. Punches 6. Point
　　9. Hammer 11. Drag ('cockscomb') 12, 13. Chisels (hammerhead)
　　14. Quirk 15, 16, 18. Chisels (mallet-head) 17. Drag 19. Riffler
　　20. Modelling tool 21. Axe-dresser 22. 'Stability' tool 23. Claw tool
　　24. Claw tool with detachable head 25. Head for (24), reversible
　　26. Boaster 27. Rubbing-weight (All 1/6, except 25, which is 1/3)

Norman Scarfe* has referred to its use at Colchester, by the
Romans for the town walls, and by the Normans in building the
Castle. Orford Castle in Suffolk is a much-quoted example, and it is
seen to great effect at the Abbey of St Osyth in Essex, where it has
been used to form a chequer pattern alternately with freestone.

Chalk has been much used, either as blocks cut to size, or
puddled; flint has in the past provided the material for many
cottages, houses and churches, sometimes dressed (but by the
flint-knapper, not the stonemason), often without preliminary dressing. The shelly deposit known as Crag has included use as building
material amongst its many services to mankind; at least two
church towers in Suffolk, built of this material, have withstood
the elements for many centuries. The Romans found it necessary
to bond flint walls with courses of tiles; many cottages of the
later periods are built of a combination of flint and brick. For the
larger buildings, however, such as churches and castles, good stone
was used whenever it was obtainable, and in any case it was
necessary for the quoins and the tracery of the windows. Moreover, the elaborate carvings which adorn our churches and
mansions could only be carried out in stone.

As a building material, stone has largely given way latterly to

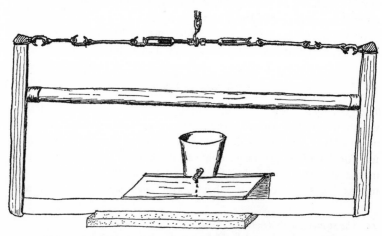

22 Stonemason's frame saw. Water is dripped from the bucket on to sand
sprinkled on the ramp. This 'lubricates' the saw as it cuts through the
stone. The blade is toothless. (Scale: 1/24)

* Norman Scarfe, *Essex, A Shell Guide*, Faber and Faber, 1968, p. 24.

concrete, but the stonemason still finds work to do; nowadays, it is more and more concerned with repairs and replacement of worn stonework; atmospheric pollution has increased to such a degree that many fine carvings would be lost if steps were not taken to arrest the decay. Accurate copying of the old work calls for a degree of skill, if not of creative talent, comparable with that of the original sculptor. Graveyard memorials, too, keep the stonemason busy, in spite of the great increase in the practice of cremation.

Another task formerly performed by the stonemason has now passed virtually into past history; he it was who used to fashion the millstones, of millstone grit, or later of French burr-stone; as the mills cease to grind, the need for the stones is no more.

Strangely, if the nature of the work of the stonemason has changed, the tools have not, in any marked degree. Perhaps the most notable loss in this respect is the huge saw with which the stone was formerly cut to size. The stone left the quarry in the form of gigantic blocks, each of such a size that it took a large transporter, drawn by two horses, to bring it to the yard. A frame saw was suspended by a chain from a pulley, and lowered on to the stone; behind it stood a low platform, on which was placed a bucket of water. A ramp led down to the level of the stone, and on this was scattered sand. A faucet in the bucket allowed water to drip slowly, carrying with it the sand, and thus assisting the friction of the blade, which was without teeth, and some four inches wide. Two of these saws, respectively eight feet and five feet in length, only recently ceased to be used in a Suffolk stonemason's yard, the smaller being operated by one man doing a twelve-hour stint. A saw of eleven feet was at one time used in a Norfolk yard. These have now been superseded by powered implements, and in any case the stone is cut to convenient sizes before delivery.

Lifting could be performed by means of a claw not unlike that used for removing the upper millstone for dressing, or with the *lewis*. A hole was bored into the upper surface of the stone, and into this was inserted a bit, often of wood with an iron lip, so constructed that it would open within the hole, thus giving a purchase for lifting by means of a pulley or crane.

Splitting was carried out by boring a hole, inserting two wedges, and driving in a bit between them.

Most processes concerned with shaping and dressing the stone are carried out with hand implements intended to be struck with either a mallet or a hammer; the head of the tool varies in form according to the striking implement to be used. For the mallet, the head is rounded, rather like a small mushroom; for use with the hammer it is flat, like that of a cold chisel, spreading out after constant use.

The mallet has a head of beechwood, although a smaller mallet, with a head of more slender build, may be of metal, often brass. There seems to be an odd lack of communication between the makers and the users of the hammer, which is invariably made with a handle of some nine or ten inches, and just as invariably cut down by the mason to four inches or even less, so that it does not swing round and impede the work.

Hammers of various sizes and weights are used, and in cutting an inscription, for instance, the side rather than the end of the head is used, but each man has his own way of working.

To prepare the surface for working, it is scraped with the *drag*, a flat plate of steel with a toothed edge; various shapes are used, and the teeth vary in size according to the degree of fineness intended. In a set of drags examined, one was seen to be nothing more nor less than a broken piece of rip-saw blade. After treatment with the *drag*, the stone was further smoothed with the *rubber* or *rubbing-weight*, a heavy cast-iron slab, the top hollowed to allow of the incorporation of two transverse bars; a pole was laid along the length of the weight and attached by binding to the two bars; it could then be pushed to and fro across the surface of the stone. This method is now of course no longer used.

Many of the chisels and other tools were made from discarded implements, and not infrequently by the mason himself, who would have a small forge for the purpose; a worn chisel would be drawn out, and perhaps an extra piece *laid* on. In other cases this service was performed by a smith, who would collect as much as a hundredweight of tools and take them away for rehabilitation.

There is a tool to cope with every situation. Stone is cut to shape (as for instance the head of a gravestone), with the *pitching-tool*, with an expanded blade with a slight inclination from the plane of the shaft. The *boaster* is somewhat similar, but with the blade in the same plane as the shaft, and like the chisels and points, is used for tooling. A tool of much the same type, the *stability chisel*, was made with a detachable bit, but this did not find favour with the working mason, and is now rarely seen. The *claw tool*, with teeth of varying size, is also sometimes made with a detachable bit. A curious implement, the *axe-dresser*, consists of a number of flat blades held in a clamp. When a pattern is worked in relief, the edges are cleared with the *riffler*, which has a triangular blade at each extremity, with a rasp surface; the *quirk* is also used for cleaning out mouldings.

Some modern chisels have a tungsten point, to cope with granite and other stones of exceptional hardness. A distinction is made between the *punch*, used with a hammer, for rough work, and the *point*, mallet-headed, for finer work.

The mason will have recourse to power-driven tools for finishing off a surface, but in general his work is still that of the true craftsman, depending on manual dexterity.

X
Rope Making

You shall never want rope enough.

FRANÇOIS RABELAIS, 1495–1553

The frequency with which the name 'Rope Walk' occurs as a street name is an indication of the extent to which this craft flourished in the past; most of the works have long since disappeared. The rope-walk at Haverhill in Suffolk is one of the very few survivors in East Anglia. As in the case of some other crafts (e.g. rake-making), some degree of mechanization has occurred, but basically the process remains as it was hundreds of years ago.

Length is one of the principal requirements, and the present rope-walk is housed in a series of ex-Army barrack huts acquired at the end of the Great War of 1914–18. They take the place of a long low shed which was entirely open to the weather on the south side, closed to the north, where light was admitted by means of what the owner described as 'a kind of port-hole, pushed out and supported on a lump of wood'.

The building is 312 feet in length; a 60-yard cord is made, and to allow for the inevitable shortening which results from the twisting together of the strands at least 80 to 85 yards is needed; then an allowance must be made for the length of the machine which effects the twisting, and of the *cart* or *jack* to which the cords are attached at the other end of the walk.

The first process is the spinning of the yarn; this is made from hemp or jute; the machinery is not suitable for the use of sisal, and the works do not go in for the manufacture of the heavier cables.

The yarn is first combed on a hackle board, a wooden block from which project a number of iron spikes. As the yarn becomes smoother, it is transferred from a board with long spikes to one on which the spikes are shorter, and so on through a series. It is treated with oil or grease to facilitate softening.

The actual spinning was formerly work for a man and a boy; the man would wrap the hemp round his waist in a *strick* (in East Anglia; *streak* elsewhere). The ends were attached to a wheel turned by a boy, and was twisted as it was paid out by the man, who shuffled backwards, paying out with one hand and smoothing with the other. The process was repeated until three lengths of yarn had been made, of the required length, one hundred yards.

The ends of the three yarns were then attached to hooks on the *twisting wheel*; this has twelve light hooks and nine heavier hooks, these last little used at Haverhill, where no thick ropes were generally made. The three yarns were twisted together to form a strand. Three, or sometimes four strands were twisted to form a line. If the yarn had been made with a clockwise twist, the strand would be twisted anti-clockwise, and the final twist to form the rope would again be clockwise.

Before twisting, the strands were laid out on the floor, and picked up with a *parting-stick*, a flat, slightly curved wooden bar, on the concave edge of which were penannular slots with which the strand was caught up, so that the separate lengths were not tangled. They were thus lifted over arms fitted with pegs to separate the strands; these were, in one series, hinged to the wall, with others running down the centre of the room. At the far end, the strands were hooked to a *cart* or *jack*, which kept the necessary tension. As the rope was made and shortened by twisting, the jack was drawn forward on a track. A short way from the jack, a *top*, a wooden cone with three grooves to part the strands, was inserted to ensure the right tension. Weights placed on the platform of the jack could steady the rate of its forward progress, upon which depended the hardness of the rope. Ropes for different purposes needed different degrees of suppleness or hardness. The greater the steadying pressure placed on the jack, the harder the *lay* of the rope.

An example of the degree of hardness which may be developed is well shown in the making of the *hand-pack*. This is a length of rope of about one yard, tapered, and with a loop at the thicker end; the lay is so hard that it may be held at the thin end, and will stand out rigid. Its use is as follows:

The fenland ploughman does not guide his horse by reins, but by word of command, as is indeed the usual practice in ploughing. A light line, the *whip-line* is attached to the bridle, and at the other end to the thin end of the *hand-pack*. If the horse shows a reluctance to obey, a sharp flick of the whip-line will serve as a reminder.

The making of a clothes-line called for a special finish; the line was polished. For this purpose a size was made from sago-flour; this was mixed into a paste, and boiling water was poured on, and the mixture thoroughly stirred. A donkey was now called into service, the end of the line being hitched to his harness; as our informant put it, 'The donkey provided the motive power'. The donkey set off down the walk, pulling the line behind him; the man would grip the line with a *bass*, a pad of coir soaked in the size, and as the cord passed through his hand it was polished. At the end of the walk man and donkey would turn and repeat the process in reverse on the next line, and so on. When the line had dried out, it was picked up in *rings* looped over the arm and reeled into *hanks*.

It has already been noted that spinning of the yarn has been discontinued at Haverhill; it is 'imported' from Dundee. The yarn is received in *chains*, made by passing loop through loop along its whole length, a convenient method of packing for transport. Arriving at the rope works, the chains are pulled out and reeled ready for use as required.

Some spinning is, however, still carried out to meet specific orders; this is of horse-hair, which was at one time much used throughout the region. Until very recently, horse-hair was woven at Glemsford, to supply the reinforcement used by tailors, e.g. in the making of jackets.

In order to keep up a steady flow of work, some sidelines are undertaken. Nets are made, in which fodder is suspended so that cattle may drag it out as needed. From time to time, too, sacks have been stitched for the coal-merchant, but the introduction of polythene has decreased the demand for these. At the time of a recent visit to the rope works, one man was busily engaged in repairing a large elephant tent for a travelling circus.

There will always, presumably, be some demand for ropes, but already the problem looms of getting sufficient work to keep the necessary skilled workers in full employment.

XI
The Maritime Crafts

The sea hath fish for every man
Sixteenth-century saying

A region with a coastline as extensive as that of East Anglia will find itself naturally concerned to exploit such an asset, both for profit and for recreation. This entails amongst other things the building of boats, for the use both of those who wish purely for the enjoyment of sailing, and those whose business or pleasure it is to catch fish and the other creatures which inhabit the sea. Boat-building and the manufacture of the sails with which the wind is harnessed for their propulsion have long passed out of the category of crafts, although their production involves the employment of craftsmen. It may therefore be felt that an account of these industries has no place in a book concerned with the traditional crafts of the region. There are, however, some activities within this sphere which are still rightfully to be included.

NET-MAKING

Many inshore fishermen still make their own nets, and around our coast others are to be found who find the work a useful sideline which can fill in the odd moments when their regular work allows. This is the case with Mr W. G. Upcraft, who combines the duties of harbour-master with those of ship-chandler at Southwold, in Suffolk, where he ministers to the needs of the local fishermen

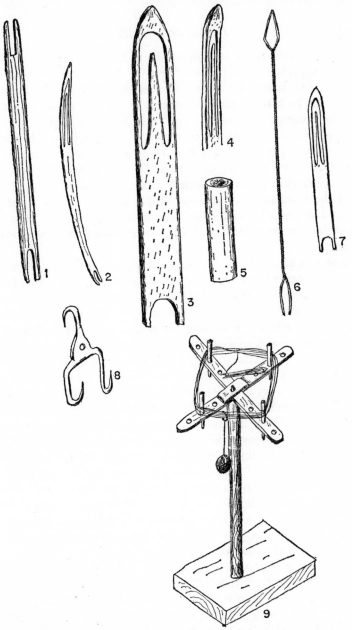

23 *Implements used in Net making and Mending*
1. Braiding needle   2, 3, 4, 6, 7. Beating needles, different sizes for
different gauges; (6) is for a shrimp net   5. Shale   8. Beatsters' hook;
hitched over a rail on the wall, to support the net during mending
9. Beatsters' *blades*; to carry a supply of thread   (No. 9 : 1/18;
remainder : 1/6)

and yachtsmen; twine and needles lie to hand where they can be picked up whenever other work permits. Nets are made, and repaired, very largely for 'part-timers and weekenders'. The inshore boats use both otter-trawls – a miniature version of those in use by the ocean-going trawlers – and beam nets; nowadays a net for a ten-ton beam is pretty well the limit, though it is only some twenty years since nets for a twenty-foot beam were made locally. Shrimp nets are also made. Of course, the nets for the regular trawlers are all now factory-made.

If the tools are comparatively simple in form, they call for as great a degree of skill for their successful use as the more numerous and more complicated implements found in many other crafts.

The process used in net-making is known as *braiding*, and is normally carried out with the *braiding needle*, a flat length of wood or bone forked at either end, so that it acts as a *bobbin* for the twine; some makers (among them W. G. Upcraft) prefer to use the *beating needle* for making the net; it is intended rather for repair work.

For many net-makers, indeed, the true braiding needle would seem to be an unknown quantity, and the writer has had pointed out to him a series in which the only distinction made was in size, the larger needles of ten inches to one foot in length being designated *braiding needles*, and those of smaller size as *beating needles*. One fisherman, with a lifetime of seagoing behind him, pointed out a beating needle with a slender waist as probably meriting the title of *braiding*. As this approach can only lead to confusion in the minds of those who, like the writer, are seeking information on traditional usage, and not intending to take up the craft themselves, for present purposes we shall reserve the term braiding needle for the open-ended form, and proceed with a description of the other variety.

It is of more elaborate form than the braiding needle; it consists essentially of a flat bar, forked at one end only, the other extremity ending in a blunt point, in some cases with a slight curve upwards, for ease in threading it through the loops of twine. It has a median slot within which is a long, slender peg, the twine passing round this on either side and round the distal fork. It may be made of any suitable wood, such as beech or ash, or of bone; how much more authentic as a medium for plying this craft than the plastic, moulded needles now common. In former times it was no uncommon sight to see a fisherman fashioning a needle with his jack-knife as he sat aboard his boat or strolled along the quay.

The size of needle used naturally varies according to the size of mesh to be formed, but as a further aid to uniformity the *shale** is used. This consists of a cylindrical block of wood or brass, or sometimes a flat square plate of wood. It is held in the palm of the left hand, the twine passing round it as each mesh is made. The size, of course, varies according to the size of the mesh. Accuracy is important; the laws against using nets which can hold fish below the permitted sizes are stringent.

The type of twine used, again varying in thickness according to need, has changed completely in recent years. Formerly a variety of materials were in use – cotton largely for herring and mackerel, especially for the drifters, manila for trawl-nets (or sisal, which was less costly); hemp for the *head-ropes, foot-ropes* and *long-ropes*. In these days of synthetic fibre, nylon has practically taken over; it has certain advantages which outweigh its shortcomings, perhaps the chief being that it is no longer necessary to make provision for spreading out the nets carefully to dry, so as to

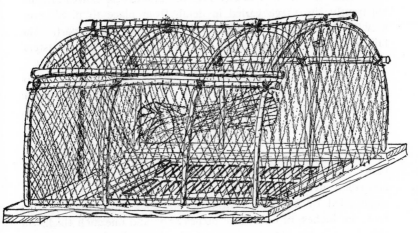

24 A Crab-pot (Scale: 1/6)

* A search for this meaning of the word in the dictionaries will prove unavailing. A. O. D. Claxton, *The Suffolk Dialect of the Twentieth Century*, Adlard, 1968, p. 68, defines it as 'the mesh of a net'. In Norfolk it may be called 'bobble'.

prevent rotting. Against this, however, must be set the fact that nylon has a tendency to slip on itself, and to form twists which are difficult to unravel, particularly in the thinner grades; it must not be left for long periods exposed to the sun, or other sources of heat, or it will disintegrate. This has been known to occur when nylon was used on a winch, due to the friction generated.

Different sections of the net call for different sizes of mesh, so must be made separately and united on completion; the *cod end*, which has to be opened for the extraction of the catch, is of very fine twine.

Storm and tempest, floating wreckage, and submerged obstructions, as well as regular wear and tear, constantly cause damage to the nets, and this must be repaired with as little delay as possible. At sea, every member of the crew can lend a hand if need be, but this is not enough, and when the vessel returns to port, the nets are taken ashore and handed to the *beatsters* – the name is self-explanatory. In the days of the peak of the herring fishery, the beatsters were organized in teams, each under a supervisor. A supply of twine was held on a machine, the *blades*, rather like an outsize wool-winder; from this the beatsters replenished their needles. This was at any rate the practice at Lowestoft, but apparently the usage varied in detail from place to place, even between Lowestoft and Kessingland, some four miles apart.* The failure of the herring harvest spelt closure to the beatsters' chambers.

Another style of net-making is demonstrated by the crab-fisherman, who makes his own *crab-pots*. As for other nets, natural twine has given way to man-made fibre. Nylon is sometimes used, but is found to be more expensive than a Portuguese product – corline – which is now in general use for this purpose.

The base of the pot is formed round a heavy cast-iron perforated plate, which serves the dual purpose of giving a firm foundation and sufficient weight to carry the pot to the sea-bed. The plate is surrounded by a frame, measuring one foot, six inches, by one foot, ten inches, of oak, three inches wide and one inch thick. On this base is erected the pot – 'built like a house', to use the fisherman's own words – but in fact rather resembling a Nissen hut, with a rounded outline formed by four hoops of cane (formerly hazel); hazel is still used for the ridge-pole, and the

* Robert Malster, *in litt.*

eaves. One side of the roof is made to open, for the removal of the catch.

For the making of the netting which covers the sides and top, a *beating-needle* of the usual type is used, but the net-maker rejects the aid of a *shale* to regulate the size of mesh. The twine is simply looped round the fingers, and the absolute accuracy achieved is something to marvel at. In one pot examined, the squares were of one inch precisely, without a fraction of variation. The netting is made in sections; for the *window* (the net-maker's term for the sides) and gable, twenty rounds, with a depth of seven rounds; for the roof, fifteen rounds; and for the *crinney*, the opening in the sides forming a tunnel for the entry of the crabs, thirteen rounds. This tunnel is open at the bottom, to allow the crabs to fall through into the pot.

The crab-pot can also be used for lobsters, though other forms are sometimes used. An entirely different pot is used for catching whelks, an occupation to which the crab-fisherman turns when the crab season is over; this is a low octagonal frame of iron, in shape rather like a pumpkin, and instead of netting, the sides are woven with rope, with a narrow neck of netting.

Fishermen, whether their quarry be pelagic swimmers or shell-fish, tend to fall into the general pattern of craftsmen, following their fathers and grandfathers, with the same pride in achievement and disregard of the hardships and hazards involved.

Overfishing has set limits to the available harvest of the sea, and to the activities of the inshore fishermen; their numbers have dwindled lamentably. Small otter- and beam-trawl nets are still in some demand, and although the drifter fleet is no more, a few longshoremen still use the drift net in the herring season, attaching it to a buoy and paying it out from the boat. Sprats are also caught, though in less quantity than formerly; the draw-nets formerly used from beach to boat have been largely put out of action by the 'dragon's teeth' and other relics of the last war.

THE FISH-CURER

To those who can appreciate the quality of a kipper or bloater smoked in the truly traditional manner, it is a sad fact that, if present trends continue, this will soon be a purely legendary pleasure. There are still a few small smokehouses dotted here and there along the East Anglian coast, but they are mainly kept going by the individual longshoreman, or the small fishmonger. Increasingly, the product appearing on the fishmonger's slabs owe their handsome bronzing to a dye, and not to the smoke of oak chips. The information on which this chapter is based was obtained from a fish-curer, one of a very small number of those practising the craft to the extent of supplying the retailer, and he was on the point of retirement. Fortunately, and due in some measure to the interest of a conservation society, a successor has been found, and the tradition will be carried on.

East Anglia has a long coastline, and fifty years ago every township, small or large, along the whole of its length, had its smokehouses.

As in the case of other crafts, the business tended to be a family affair; the expertise demanded thus passed from father to son; the knowledge was almost inborn, for in the case of our informant a beginning was made at the age of eight years, the first task being the making of boxes in which the kippers were packed when ready for sale. The necessity for this was recognized to such an extent that the boy was allowed to appear at school half an hour late each morning, and to leave half an hour before the rest of the class. At thirteen and a half he was able to leave school and enter the business full-time, at the princely wage of 2s. 6d. a week. Meantime, he was gaining knowledge and experience by accompanying his father to the fish market, to learn the finer points of buying to ensure a supply of the finest herring; only the best were good enough for smoking. In another three years he was doing all the buying. Small wonder that, with such an intensive training, he not only acquired a special skill which could only be gained in this way, but also that complete confidence in his own ability, and pride in achievement, that is the mark of the true craftsman.

Any fish can be smoked; in addition to the herring, which formed the bulk of the material, haddock, cod, whiting, pollack and plaice were all acceptable. Plaice smoked well; sole presented more of a problem, as if smoked for too long it became leathery. Salmon, trout of various kinds, and other freshwater fish – all were tried. Cod and haddock were all obtained locally; their quality was dependent to some extent on where they were caught – in fact, on the source of their food. Eels needed a very thorough smoking until they were partly cooked, and even then could not compete with those from Holland, where a special technique seems to have been developed which has not so far been mastered in this country.

In the days when the East Anglian herring fishery was at its best, the season for smoking began with local fish, bought in the market by the *cran*, a measure of about thirty-seven and a half imperial gallons (according to the dictionary), amounting to approximately seven hundred to a thousand fish, depending on the size. When local sources were exhausted, as the shoals moved southward, stocks were obtained from the south coast, at Ramsgate and Milford. Then the source moved to the north, to Scotland – Lerwick, Peterhead and Fraserburgh; then to North Shields; to Grimsby; and so to the local fisheries again. With a lull of a couple of months or so, a circuit of the British Isles kept up the supply. In addition, what were described as 'quality herring' came from Norway, and were much prized.

The smokehouses varied in size from those dealing with three or four crans at a time to large houses which can take up to one hundred crans.

For kippers, the smoke is produced by burning shavings of oak or ash, preferably: for bloaters, billets of oak are used. Apple wood, when obtainable, gives a distinctive flavour.

Several factors must be taken into account to get the right results. Both the degree of 'brining' and the length of actual smoking depend on whether the fish is to be prepared for quick sale, or will need to be kept for some time. The weather, too, and especially the direction and force of the wind, will have an effect.

The smokehouse has a 'stable' door, with separate top and bottom halves; the top is closed, and the bottom left open to maintain the draught. The fires are lit, and when burning vigorously, are damped down with dust; the flame is 'killed' to increase the volume of smoke.

To prepare the herring for kippering, an incision is made down the ventral surface from head to tail; the fish is then laid open, and the gills and gut removed. An essential part of the process is the scraping of the bone, removing any blood, as this when burnt would produce a black or reddish streak which is considered a mark of bad workmanship.

The fish is then well washed with fresh water, and placed in a brine made from rock salt, coarse, of grains about the size of a pea. The length of time allowed for brining is a matter for careful judgment, and is related to the ultimate destination of the fish. A short time only is needed if it is intended for sale locally, much longer if it is to go for export, possibly to Australia, Canada or America, as many did in the hey-day of the craft.

After drying, the herring is ready for smoking. For this, the fish are hung on hooks on the *baulks*, which are fixed to the racks or *horses* in the smokehouse. Here again the time element depends on the interval which is expected to elapse before the fish is to be sold for the table. Some idea of the time required for quick sale may be given; if the weather is good, with a fair wind, kippering might be completed in about four hours. Then 'you could take the bottoms off', that is to say, the lower layers can be removed from their baulks, and hung on racks to cool off before packing into boxes. According to the conditions of wind and weather, the smoking may be uneven – fronts satisfactorily smoked, but backs needing further treatment. In such a case, the fires are relit, and the process repeated.

Bloaters are smoked whole, not opened. This requires the steadier heat obtained when billets, not shavings are burnt; otherwise the method is the same, and calls for the same degree of judgment on the part of the operator.

The natural kipper, smoked by the expert, was calculated to satisfy the senses of sight, smell and taste. In this artificial age, when even sun-tan comes out of a bottle, the pleasant golden-brown of the true kipper has been replaced by a vegetable dye which fails dismally to reproduce its qualities; smell and taste, too, are feeble imitations of the real thing.

The disappearance of the smokehouse from the local scene is due in large part to the decline of the herring fishery, but also to the fact that, although the apparatus is simple and the tools of the trade few by comparison with those of the wheelwright, blacksmith, cooper and others, production can no longer be maintained on a scale which will provide a living wage for the fish curer.

XII

The Miller & the Millwright

. . . more water glideth by the mill
Than wots the miller of
SHAKESPEARE, *Titus Andronicus*

Of all the regions of this country, East Anglia may surely claim to share with Holland the title of 'the land of mills'. It does not merit the description so frequently applied; it is by no means 'flat'. It has however no towering mountains to interrupt the even flow of the wind, and it has those gentle eminences which can be used to site the windmill to gain the full benefit of every breeze. It is intersected by streams which may be harnessed to turn the wheel of the watermills, and it has tidal estuaries on which, in times past, numbers of tidemills took advantage of the ebb and flow of the tides.

The mills served a variety of purposes; perhaps that which, for the majority of people, comes most readily to mind, is the grinding of corn to make flour, and again, no other region can more fully illustrate the evolution of the practice. The saddle-quern of the Neolithic Period derives its name from the form it assumed as a result of the fore-and-aft motion of the rubbing stone; it was followed in the Bronze and Iron Ages by the rotary-querns, and these, in one form or another, persisted in some of the more remote regions of these islands until quite recent times. The Romans introduced a type more resembling in form the later millstones, of Andernach lava from the Rhineland,* but found it unnecessary to go to the trouble of continuing to import them, as the grit-stones from the Peak District of Derbyshire (later to be known as *millstone* grit), and the hard conglomerate called *puddingstone*, from the appearance due to the mass of pebbles welded together in a matrix of finer grain, proved to be equal, if not superior to the lavas for the purpose. Millstone grit remained the usual material for millstones, at least in East Anglia, until well into the nineteenth century, when it was gradually supplanted by *French burr-stone* quarried in the Paris area. Even then stones of this material were reserved for milling wheat, Millstone grit being retained for barley, for feeding stuffs.†

French burr-stone occurs in small blocks, of which a number have to be cemented together to form a millstone; the stone is then bound with an iron hoop. It has the merit that it can take a much finer degree of dressing than other stones; it is very hard, and will not only wear longer, but develop less grit in the flour.

Our concern is with mills and milling in East Anglia, and it would be superfluous to give a detailed account of the manner in which the mill is made to harness the forces of nature, wind and water, to perform the tasks desired. This has been done in many books,‡ but some account must be given of the way in which mills have been made to meet the needs of the region.

The earliest mills seem to have been watermills, and it is not until the twelfth century that a windmill is recorded in England,§ and that not in our region. In later times, however, watermills and windmills worked in pairs, so that the miller could take advantage of wind or current as was most opportune. The only remaining evidence of this practice is at Pakenham, in Suffolk, where the tower-mill has been restored and is in working order, and the adjoining watermill has just ceased working. Efforts are in progress to save this mill from destruction (or conversion to a dwelling as had been proposed). The two have, of course, for long been in separate ownership, but their proximity makes it virtually certain that they were at one time paired.

Much interest has been aroused in recent years in the mills

* I. A. Richmond, *Roman Britain*, Pelican Books, 1955, p. 169.
† N. Smedley, *The Alton Watermill*, Friends of the Abbot's Hall Museum, p. 17.
‡ Notably John Reynolds' *Windmills and Watermills*, Hugh Evelyn, 1970.
§ *Op. cit.*, p. 69.

which remain to us, but for the most part only windmills lend themselves to restoration. If restoration *in situ* is impossible, removal and re-erection is a possible alternative, and this was adopted in the case of the Alton Watermill in Suffolk. The site was to be submerged to form a reservoir, and a condition laid down when permission was eventually given to proceed with the scheme was that the watermill should be moved to the Abbot's Hall Museum of Rural Life of East Anglia at Stowmarket, where the present writer was engaged in forming what was, it was then hoped, to be an Open Air Museum fully representing of the region, and comparable with those in Scandinavia and the Netherlands and Belgium. An account of the operation has been given in a small publication issued by the Museum;* both the mill and its associated buildings had many points of special interest.

Of the watermills, both those with the *undershot* wheel, in which the water flows beneath the wheel, thus exerting pressure on the *floats*,† and causing the wheel to turn, and the *overshot* wheel and its variant the *breast-shot* wheel, in both of which the water strikes the wheel from above, turning it in the reverse direction, were used in East Anglia. The type selected depended on the character of the stream, but wherever possible it seems to have been the practice to use the *overshot* wheel, which was more effective.

The flow of water was regulated by sluice-gates, and where a river served a succession of mills in its length, the interruption of the flow occasionally led to dispute between one miller and his immediate neighbour. The possession of a sluice-gate had its perquisites. Eels on their way to their breeding-grounds in the distant ocean could be diverted from the main course of the river and made to pass through the sluice. One Norfolk innkeeper used to make an annual visit to a nearby Suffolk mill, to set a net in position, and so intercept the shoals of eels.

Where a river was tidal it was possible to take advantage of the fact to operate a watermill. The incoming tide filled the mill-pool, and the mill functioned during the period of the ebb-tide. The one disadvantage was, of course, this absolute reliance on the tides,

* N. Smedley, *The Alton Watermill*, Friends of the Abbot's Hall Museum, 1974.
† Rather oddly so-called; most of them have long since ceased to be made of wood, which has been replaced with iron.

and more than ever was the practice of the paired mills brought into play. Essex was particularly well provided with tide-mills, and many of these were partnered with windmills.* Unlike the mills of Norfolk, Suffolk and Cambridgeshire, which catered very largely for the needs of the surrounding areas, the Essex mills, and especially the 'paired mills' of the estuaries and tidal rivers, were favourably placed for the London trade. Some of the millers themselves owned vessels for the transport of the grain to London. Many of them, too, owned their own farms, and so were particularly well equipped for the trade.

All this is now a thing of the past; the last of the watermills has ceased to grind either for flour or meal, though only within very recent years.

Although the grinding of corn was the principal function of the mills, a profitable sideline developed in the hey-day of the wool trade, that of fulling the cloth for the wool merchants; this was actually carried out in the corn-mills, although a number of mills appear in the records as 'fulling mills'. During the decline of the wool trade during the eighteenth century the mills gradually reverted to flour production, but in one case it would seem that the involvement with the textile trade led to a reversal of the general trend. The watermill at Syleham, on the Suffolk bank of the Waveney which separates that county from Norfolk, whilst retaining its character as a corn-mill, supplied power for the spinning of cotton, and the weaving of a material for the manufacture of clothing for farm-workers, *drabette*, which was also produced by the Haverhill family of Gurteen. At Syleham, the waterwheel was also used to provide power for sewing machines for the manufacture of clothing, and continued to do so until the mill was burnt down in 1928, when the work was carried on using other sources of power.

The windmill, as has been seen, was introduced to give an alternative to water power. An impetus was given to the building of more windmills by the introduction, in the eighteenth century, of restrictions on the building of new watermills (which was also responsible for an increase in the number of tide-mills), and by the comparatively low cost of building them. The choice of sites was governed by two main factors, the need for the mill to be in

* A. F. J. Brown, *Essex at Work 1700–1815*, Essex Record Office Publications, No. 49, 1969, pp. 57–9.

as close proximity as possible to the watermill, if it was one of a pair, and the necessity to place it where it would get a free current of air to turn the sails. In a region where the contour of the land is low, advantage was taken of any rise in the ground, and as a result windmills became prominent features of the landscape. To William Cobbett, writing in 1829, they were 'the most beautiful sight of the kind that I have ever beheld'.* To many a traveller, they formed landmarks invaluable in a region intersected by innumerable winding lanes.

Windmills were of three main types. The post-mill predominated in East Anglia, probably because, being constructed principally of timber, it was quickly and easily built, and could as easily be dismantled and removed to another site, if this proved desirable. It was built on a stout post, supported by a substructure of cross-beams and transverse stays;† in most cases, this framework was later enclosed in a round-house of brick, which served both as a protection and a store. The whole body of the mill revolved on the top of the post, as required, to face into the wind. Steps led down to within a foot or so of the ground, and also supported a *tail-pole*, ending in a wheel which ran round a track to facilitate the turning process, at first carried out by hand, but generally later by the addition of a *fantail*, a kind of miniature set of sails which automatically brought the *buck*, or body, round into the wind. In the case of one Suffolk post-mill, that at Drinkstone, the fantail was added by the present owner, Wilfred Clover, the *fly-post* coming from the dismantled mill at Woolpit, close by, and the *fan* from farther afield, at Stradbroke. The round-house had been added by his great-great-grandfather.

The earlier type of sail used, the *common sail*, was in very truth a sail, for it was sheeted with canvas. This allowed the speed to be checked by taking in a reef, a procedure which could be difficult and even dangerous in a strong wind, as the mill had to be stopped, and each sail lowered in turn, to effect it. A later development was the *shuttered sail*, fitted with a series of spring-loaded louvres which could be closed or opened according to the force of the wind.

The tower-mill is a much more permanent structure than the post-mill, in which the machinery is accommodated in a brick-built tower, only the cap, bearing the sails, revolving into the wind with the aid of a fantail.

A version of the tower-mill, the smock-mill, works on the same principle, but the tower is of timber construction, with eight sides. It is characteristic of the Netherlands, from where it was probably introduced into this country.

Windmill or watermill, post-mill or tower-mill or smock-mill, the principle is the same; a horizontal force, wind or water, activates a turning mechanism revolving in a vertical plane. This force has then to be converted by a series of geared wheels, back into the horizontal plane.

Another means of turning the stones to grind the grain was the horse-mill, in which a horse, harnessed to a long shaft, simply rotated the stones. A mill of this type operated at Drinkstone, within a stone's throw of the post-mill, in a 'round-house' with sixteen sides. It was later converted into an octagonal smock-mill, by the addition of a superstructure. Later still, after the collapse of the sails, it was operated by a small engine, a form of power which extended the lease of life of many mills, both wind- and water-. Such an engine was installed at the Alton Watermill, though apparently the anticipated failure of the water supply never materialized, and the engine was never brought into use. With the introduction of competition from the rolling-mills in the latter part of the nineteenth century, a small rolling-mill was built to supplement the work of the watermill at Wickham Market.

Many farms possessed a small *stone-mill*, a pair of stones set up in the corner of a barn or other outbuilding, and powered by a *horsework* (which had many other uses on the farm), or a stationary engine or later a tractor.

Another use for mills was the drainage of the marshes; most of these *wind-pumps* take the form of small tower-mills, but one Norfolk wind-pump is of the post-mill type, and that at Herringfleet (formerly in Suffolk, but now transferred under the readjustment of county boundaries to Norfolk) is a smock-mill, as also is the wind-pump at Wicken Fen, in Cambridgeshire.

This country has never applied its mill power to the variety of tasks that is to be found for example in the Netherlands, where both windmills and watermills are used for the preparation of oil, for papermaking, and as timber sawmills.

The wool-merchants, in their day, had been esteemed as ranking high in the social scale; with the decline of the wool trade, their place in society was taken by the millers, but although the miller amassed wealth and estates, he remained very truly a craftsman whilst he continued to work. The running of the mill was very largely a one-man job, and although he may have had a man or two about the place, and an apprentice, his was the hand which, physically, controlled the mill.

Some idea of the position on the social scale of the miller in relation to those in other occupations may be gathered from the case of Edward Cooke Vincent, the son of a surgeon at Wells in Norfolk. When he proved unsuitable to follow in his father's footsteps, arrangements were made for him to be apprenticed to Amos Tiffen, the miller at Boxford in Suffolk. The indenture relating to the apprenticeship imposed a strict code of conduct on the apprentice, and an obligation on the miller to instruct him 'in the Art of a Miller and Maltster'. It is transcribed in full in an earlier book.*

In the corn-mill, the provision of a *lay-shaft* made it possible to use the available power for other purposes than the driving of the stones; machines were used for oat-crushing, and for kibbling barley and other crops; the hoist raised and lowered the sacks of corn and flour between the *lucam* (or *locum*) and the waiting wagon below. When the stones required dressing to maintain their efficiency a crane operated by this secondary mechanism raised the *runner-stone* and reversed it, so that both stones could receive attention to the grooves which allowed the ground flour to escape. At one time, stone-dressers travelled from mill to mill, but in more recent times, and perhaps usually in East Anglia, dressing was carried out by the miller himself. The implement used was the *mill-bill*, a kind of chisel-bladed pick, housed in a wooden handle, the *thrift*. For the stone of millstone grit, a series of comparatively wide, shallow grooves divided the stone into ten sectors. The grooves ran at a slightly tangential angle from the centre, and were interspersed with a secondary series running diagonally. Each groove was cut vertically down on the side which would meet the

* Norman Smedley, *Life and Tradition in Suffolk and North-East Essex*, Dent, 1976, p. 138.

grain as the stone turned, and sloped on the other side. French burr-stones could take a finer cut, with additional grooves running inside the primary and secondary series. The level of the surface was tested from time to time with a straight-edge.

If versatility and a capacity for hard work and long hours were characteristics demanded of the miller, even more was required of the millwright, who designed mills, installed the machinery, and attended to the correction of any faults which might develop in the course of use. He had to be something of an architect, and a great deal of an engineer.

Many factors govern the choice of site for a mill, whether wind- or water-. The foundations must be sound; the structure will be subject to considerable stress, especially in the case of the wind-mill. It is necessary to have a knowledge of conditions natural to the area, prevailing winds, and the force to be expected; the flow of a stream, and whether an undershot or overshot wheel will be the more suitable; sources of materials, and accessibility of the site for transport.

Inside the mill, it will be found that a variety of materials have been used. Some wheels are of timber, others of iron; at some points these may intermesh. The care of the mill and its machinery demands the services of the wheelwright throughout its life, just as the farm needs the services of the veterinary surgeon for the care of its livestock, or the agricultural engineer for its tractors and ploughs and drills.

XIII
The Domestic Crafts

Bad men live to eat and drink, whereas good men eat and drink
in order to live.

SOCRATES (469–399 B.C.)

Hitherto we have been concerned with those crafts which are the
province of the trained craftsman. No account of the traditional
crafts of a region, however, would be complete without some
account of those which are largely carried out in the home. Unless
they are recorded now, it will be impossible to get a first-hand
account of them, for they are fast giving place to the cult of the
'ready-made'.

BAKING

The village baker has virtually disappeared from the scene,
although here and there one may be found who will provide an
alternative to the leathery substance turned out by the modern
bakery. Even so, he will use electricity or gas to heat his ovens;
where the brick oven is still to be seen, it is in a private house the
owner of which is proud to possess such a relic, and to use it from
time to time. No food cooked in modern equipment can quite
equal its products.

The usual place for the oven was the kitchen wall, and it was
built at a height convenient for firing and loading without undue
stooping; some cottages had a separate bakehouse at the rear, but

this was the exception rather than the rule. The roof was domed, to give a better distribution of the heat than would straight, angled sides, and it was easier to clean out. There was no separate fireplace; the fire was actually built inside the oven, the fuel varying according to the locality. Trimmings from the hedge, or on the heathland furze or ling, were bound into faggots before being thrust into the furnace. This is of some interest, as experiments with a replica of a Roman pottery kiln carried out some years ago showed that the uniform heat required was best attained with faggots.

Some account of this method of baking has been given by Allan Jobson* and by George Ewart Evans,† and the present writer was fortunate in being given a first-hand description of baking as carried out in the Wicken Fen area of Cambridgeshire where, as might be expected, peat cut from the Fen was used. The order of loading the oven also differed from that customary in Suffolk.

Where faggots were used, these were stacked in the oven, and the fire kindled. As the soot burned from the sides and roof, the bricks showed first red, and then, at the rear, white. When this stage was reached it was time to start baking, but some housewives would make certain by throwing in a light sprinkling of flour, which would spark if the temperature was right.

The flour was kept in a *flour hutch* or *ark*; in one Suffolk farmhouse, where rats were a problem, this was suspended from the ceiling of an upper room. Yeast was often kept back after it had been used in home-brewing (to be discussed later).

As the heating of the oven proceeded, the embers were spread by means of an *oven fork*, or sometimes an ordinary garden rake. In the interests of economy, one heating was made to serve the baking of other items besides the bread; puddings, pies, tarts and sausage-rolls went to the rear, bread to the front. The various items were placed on the *oven peel*, a flat shovel with a very long handle, also used to remove them.

In the Wicken Fen farmhouse the fire was started by placing in the front of the oven about twenty blocks of peat, each roughly a foot long by two inches square in section. These were stacked in two rows leaning against one another, rather as the rafters of

* Allan Jobson, *Household and Country Crafts*, Elek Books, 1953, pp. 24–31.
† George Ewart Evans, *Ask the Fellows who Cut the Hay*, Faber and Faber, 1956 (reprinted 1972), pp. 55–9.

a roof. When these were well alight two faggots of brushwood were added, and the fire left to burn until the rear of the oven showed white. The hot ashes were raked out, and used to heat a cauldron of water, suspended above the hearth, ready for washing-up.

Pastries and sausage-rolls went in first, when these were cooked, they were taken out, and the bread put in at the back of the oven, with a large rice pudding in front.

When the village bakehouse was still functioning it was quite usual for the local housewives to make up their own loaves, and take them along to the bakery for baking. In the case of one Suffolk village the nearest baker was on the other side of the River Waveney, in Norfolk, so the bread went into another county to be baked. In fact, however, this meant a journey of only about a quarter of a mile.

The baker's oven performed another function; the long clay pipes, known as 'churchwardens', became foul after a time. They were then placed in a *cradle*, and put into the oven to be fired to burn away the tar. This service could also be given by the blacksmith, in his forge.

BUTTER-MAKING

The craft of butter-making has largely gone the way of many country crafts, through economic considerations. With increased specialization on the farm the general practice is for the milk to be piped off from the milking-parlour direct into a tanker, which conveys it to the distributor. There is no longer a ready supply for the farmer's wife to use for making butter, curd or cheese. Where this is made, it is usually on one of the few remaining small general-purpose farms, where a few cows may be kept for the home supply. It is only in the last generation that this has come about; in the early days of the present century butter-making was encouraged; the County Councils of Norfolk and Suffolk held joint classes to promote a knowledge of dairying. In many a private house or cottage would be found one of the small table-churns, or box-churns, or an 'atmospheric churn', a tall glass jar, the lid carrying a crank which operated a rod bearing wooden paddles which projected down into the jar.

The milk was put overnight in a shallow bowl, and left for the

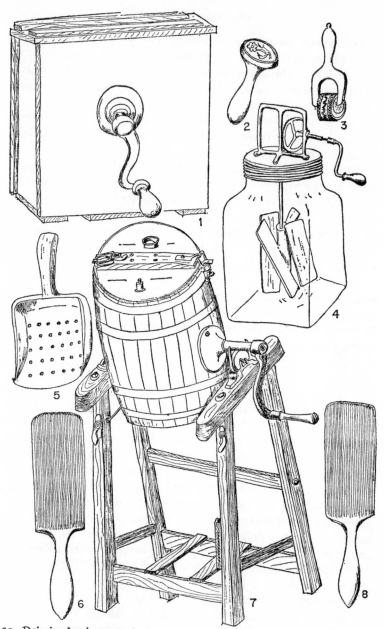

25 *Dairying Implements – I*
1. Table-churn 2, 3. Butter-stamps 4. 'Atmospheric' churn 5. Butter-scoop 6, 8. Butter-hands 7. Over-and-under churn (Nos 1, 2, 4, 5, 6 and 8: 1/6; 3: 1/3; 7: 1/12)

cream to rise. In the morning the cream was skimmed off using a *fleeter*, a shallow perforated scoop of tin, or sometimes of brass or copper. The cream was kept until enough had been accumulated to make it worth while to churn it.

The earliest churns were simply barrels fitted on a stand, horizontally, and turned by a crank. At first these were made by the cooper, but in time firms specialized in their production. *The Country Gentleman's Catalogue* for 1894 advertised a barrel-churn of triangular section, and one of these was found on a Suffolk farm recently; the shape would tend to throw the cream about more violently than the circular form, and this effect would be increased when the end-over-end churn, in which the barrel is upright, was introduced. This was the usual churn in the early years of this century; it had just been introduced when the 1894 catalogue was issued, and appears in it.

When the barrel-churn was in use the butter was washed in a *keeler*, a shallow tub on legs; the butter was squeezed in the hand, or pressed with a mushroom-shaped pestle of willow. The introduction of the end-over-end churn made the keeler redundant, as the butter could be washed in the churn by pouring in pail after pail of water. A perforated scoop, also of willow, was used to remove the butter from the churn after washing, and it was then placed in the *butter-worker*, a flat wooden trough, supported on a stand. In this it was rolled with a wooden roller, with parallel blades. In the early models this is used like a rolling-pin, manually, but in later versions it is fitted with a crank, and runs the length of the *butter-worker* on wheels. When it is free of water, the butter is worked into pound or half-pound slabs with the *butter-hands*, and may be marked with a pattern using the *butter-moulds*, sometimes round stamps, or a wheel carved with a design, or the name of the maker.*

CHEESE-MAKING

East Anglia does not produce any cheeses of outstanding note, comparable with Stilton, Cheddar, Wensleydale or Gloucester, though at one time the amount of cheese produced threatened the butter supply. This may account for the fact that it became custo-

* For some early comments on Suffolk butter and cheese, see Norman Smedley, *Life and Tradition in Suffolk and North-East Essex*, Dent, 1976, pp. 120, 121.

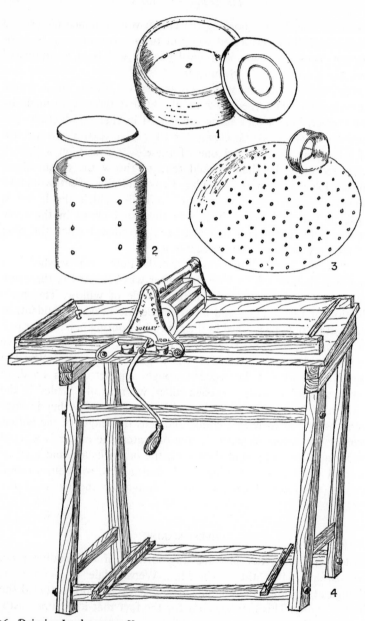

26 *Dairying Implements – II*
  1, 2. Cheese-vats 3. Fleeter 4. Butter-worker (Nos 1, 2 and 3 : 1/6;
  4 : 1/12)

mary to use the milk left after skimming to take the cream for butter-making. This again had an adverse effect on the quality of the cheese, particularly that of Suffolk. So notorious did this *Suffolk Bang* become that Robert Bloomfield, the Suffolk poet (1766–1823), waxed lyrical over it:

> *Unrivalled stands thy country Cheese, O Giles!*
> *Whose very name alone engenders smiles;*
> *Whose fame abroad by every tongue is spoke,*
> *The well-known butt of many a flinty joke . . .*
> . . . .
> *Hence Suffolk dairy-wives run mad for cream,*
> *And leave their milk with nothing but its name;*
> *Its name derision and reproach pursue,*
> *And strangers tell of 'three times skimm'd sky-blue'.*
> *To cheese converted, what can be its boast?*
> *What, but the common virtues of a post!*
> *If drought o'ertake it faster than the knife,*
> *Most fair it bids for stubborn length of life,*
> *And, like the oaken shelf whereon 'tis laid,*
> *Mocks the weak effort of the bending blade;*
> *Or in the hog-trough rests in perfect spite,*
> *Too big to swallow, and too hard to bite.*

Sometimes the quality was improved by adding to the skimmed the full-cream milk from the morning milking, and if an even better grade was intended, the cream skimmed from the first batch was added, after warming. The mixture was poured into the cooper-made *keeler* already described in the account of butter-making, salt added, and a quantity of *rennet*. In former times this was prepared in the dairy from the *vell* or third stomach of a calf; a Norfolk recipe* describes how this is done, with the addition to the rennet of the leaves of the dog rose, those of the bramble, a lemon and cloves, but certainly from the early days of the twentieth century, it could be purchased ready-made. After being stirred to break up the curd, it was strained in a muslin bag, to get rid of some of the whey, and then transferred to the *cheese-vats*, small shallow bowls of willow, with holes in the base to allow the whey to escape, and a lid which rested within the periphery of the vat. These were placed in a cheese-press, often to be found

* Smedley, *op. cit.*, pp. 121–2.

E.A.C.—K

built into the dairy or kitchen, and the cheeses were turned out when firm as circular, flat slabs. A softer *cottage cheese* is made, without the application of the same degree of pressure as is normal; goats' milk may be used for this.

As in the case of butter, however, changed conditions on the farm have reduced the opportunities for this process to be carried out.

HOME-BREWED BEER

It has become something of a craze of late to brew one's own beer; a package, with all the necessary ingredients, and full instructions, may be bought of any chemist. This is not, however, the traditional brew of the East Anglian countryside. It used to be the custom for the farmer to provide beer on the great occasions of the farming year, such as the harvest, and it was not the farmer alone who kept up the custom of the twice-yearly brew, usually in October and March.

In earlier days no licence was necessary for a householder paying an annual rent of less than £12,* and it is still possible to get a free licence where the annual value of the house is assessed at no more than £8, with the proviso that permission is limited to 'a quantity not exceeding four bushels of malt or equivalent thereof for his own use'.†

This would not, of course, meet the farmer's needs, so twice every year he bought one bushel of malt and one pound of hops; his licence cost him four shillings annually. In the early years of the century his malt and hops cost only six shillings, and made twenty gallons of beer, so that his annual expenditure was £1.

The malt was put into a keeler, which might be that also used for butter- and cheese-making, but was often one kept specially for the purpose. Two gallons of cold water were first poured, followed by one of hot, and the malt *mashed* by scooping it up with the hands to ensure that it was thoroughly wet. It was then left overnight to soak. The following morning the copper was lit, so that a supply of hot water would be ready as soon as needed. The tap or faucet of the keeler projected inside the keeler, so that a *wilsh*, a basketwork sheath, could be fitted over it, thus preventing any escape of the malt grains. Enough water was added

* Allan Jobson, *Household and Country Crafts*, Elek, 1953, pp. 45–6.
† George Ewart Evans, *Ask the Fellows who Cut the Hay*, Faber and Faber, 1956 (1972), p. 65.

to ensure that the malt was fully covered, then another gallon of boiling water from the copper was ladled in gradually, using a hand-cup made of willow, often of a single piece, the handle forming a channel. This is also to take samples for testing.

The mixture is stirred with the *masher*, a spade-like implement, the 'blade' of which has an openwork series of bars. Then the keeler is covered with the rack, which is often a naturally forked branch, over which a cloth is placed to keep in the nature of the brew.

27 *Baking and Brewing Implements*
1. Oven peel   2. Oven fork   3. Brewing funnel (*tunnel*)   4. Hand-cup, made from a single piece of willow   5. Masher   6. Faucet with *wilsh* (Nos 1, 2 and 5: 1/16; remainder: 1/6)

Now comes the time, after the liquor has steeped for about four hours, to open the tap, and allow the *wort* to run into a tub which has been placed at a lower level. More water is added to the remaining malt to form the *second wort*.

The *first wort* was boiled in the copper, and about three-quarters of the hops added, boiled for a further four hours, then drained through a sieve into the tub. The *second wort*, boiled with the remaining quarter of the hops, forms the *small beer*, or the two may be reunited to form one brew.

After cooling, a pint of yeast is added; this has been collected from a neighbour, and will be passed on to another when it has performed its task of fermenting the beer.

Meantime the casks have been thoroughly scoured; a length of chain is put into the cask, which is rolled, the chain scraping off any accumulation from the previous year. Pouring into the cask is carried out with the aid of a funnel (*tunnel*). The beer was ready for drinking at the end of the week, but was better left, and could keep perfectly for a year.

CIDER-MAKING

Out of small beginnings, firms of some note as producers of cider have sprung up in three out of the four counties of East Anglia – Bulmer of Harlow in Essex, Gaymer of Attleborough in Norfolk, and the Aspall Cyder House in Suffolk. They have developed into the sphere of industry rather than craft, and we are here concerned with the craft of cider-making, but the story of the early days of the Aspall firm is of particular interest because of its repercussions on various aspects of the life of the district.

In 1702 Temple Chevallier, of St Helier, Jersey, had succeeded to estates in the area of Suffolk which includes Aspall. He died in 1722, leaving the property to his cousin, Clement Benjamin Chevallier, a merchant of St Helier, who also ran a small cider mill. This mill, a circular stone platform with a peripheral channel in which the apples were crushed, Clement brought over and installed at Aspall. It was operated by a horse harnessed to a radial shaft. He also brought over and planted trees of the right stock, and gradually built up a considerable business. The stone mill has now, of course, been superseded by modern presses, but is demonstrated on occasion.

At the same time, Clement founded a branch of the Chevallier family whose activities had far-reaching effects on several different aspects of local life. His son Temple became rector of a number of parishes including Aspall, and, like many others of the clergy, took to farming in his no doubt considerable spare time; he became famous for his herd of dairy cattle, and research into the development of root crops, and cabbages. Temple had twelve children of whom the fifth, John, succeeded his father in the living. He was medically qualified and founded a home for patients suffering from mental diseases. His most notable contribution, however, was his discovery of a new and prolific strain of barley, which became known as 'Chevallier Barley'. He was active, too, in local politics, and took the chair at the early meetings aimed at extending the railway into Suffolk.

The traditional method of cider-making, however, was very different from that used by the Chevalliers. The type of press used has not varied in form for the last two hundred years, at least. It consists of a large tub, twenty-one inches by fifteen inches, by fourteen inches deep, flanked by two stout upright posts bearing a cross-bar through which passes the screw by which pressure is applied to the plunger which crushes the apples. The frame is of oak; the sides of the tub are lined with vertical slats of sycamore, to act as bearers for the plunger.

All the apparatus is first thoroughly scrubbed, and the barrels washed out in the same manner as were the beer barrels, inserting lengths of chain which will scour away any sediment remaining from the previous year.

For this rough cider, any apples can be used – cooking or eating varieties; the condition is of little consequence, but they should not have been sprayed, or at any rate not recently. They must be finely chopped, and traditionally this was carried out in a simple machine consisting of a shallow trough, mounted on legs, and fitted with a crank-operated spindle bearing a number of blades or spikes. More recently, some amateur cider-makers have enlisted the aid of the local butcher, who would cut up the apples in his sausage-machine. One such machine was acquired when the butcher, taken over by a larger firm, gave up making sausages; it is electrically driven, and performs the task expertly and with speed.

Before the apples are put into the tub, this is lined with a perforated mat; these were formerly of coconut fibre, but are now specially made of polythene mesh. Mats are placed at intervals between the layers of apples, to ensure a regular flow.

An earthenware bowl, with a capacity of five gallons, is placed beneath the spout of the tub; when the screw is given a turn, the flow of juice begins.

Next, the sugar is added, usually one and a half pounds to a gallon of juice, but this may be varied according to whether it is intended to make a dry or sweet cider, or something in between. The tub will produce about six gallons from one filling.

The liquid is transferred to the barrels, which are set on a stand with the bung-hole uppermost. As fermentation proceeds, foam will be formed at the opening, and a glass tube may be fitted to indicate when this is complete. The cider may be drinkable within one week, but a year is considered a suitable period to allow for full maturity.

Index

Figures in *italics* indicate illustration pages.

N.

M.

O.